Feeding Smart

with The Science Dog

Linda P. Case

Feeding Smart with The Science Dog
Linda P. Case

AutumnGold Publishing
A Division of AutumnGold Consulting
Mahomet, IL 61853
www.autumngoldconsulting.com

ISBN: 9798780285502

Other Books by Linda P. Case

Dog Smart: Evidence-based Training
with The Science Dog

Dog Food Logic: Making Smart Decisions for your Dog
in an Age of Too Many Choices

Beware the Straw Man: The Science Dog Explores Dog
Training Fact & Fiction

Canine and Feline Nutrition: A Resource for Companion
Animal Professionals (3rd Edition)

The Dog: Its Behavior, Nutrition and Health

The Cat: Its Behavior, Nutrition and Health

Canine and Feline Behavior and Training: A Complete
Guide to Understanding our Two Best Friends

To Cooper, Alice & Stanley

Table of Contents

Introduction

When dog owners are surveyed or queried directly, the majority report that they believe that proper nutrition and a healthful diet is essential for their dog's long-term health and wellness. A substantial number go so far as to say that nutrition is the *most* important factor influencing their dog's health and quality of life.

Clearly, providing optimal nutrition to our dogs is of great importance to us. Unfortunately, selecting nutritious and safe foods for our dogs is frequently more difficult to accomplish than it should be. This difficulty arises from several factors. These include the overabundance of choices that owners face on the pet food aisle, the onslaught of marketing campaigns suggesting that every new food will be the holy grail of canine health, plus an internet-driven explosion of unqualified, overstated, and sometimes outright fictitious claims about a particular nutrient, food, or feeding approach. Add in social media and the profusion of personal (and often heated) arguments regarding what dogs actually require and what feeding approach or diet is best for them and it is not surprising that dog owners find themselves throwing up their hands in frustration.

In an attempt to address these issues, my first Science Dog nutrition book, *Dog Food Logic,* took a deep dive into the science of our dogs' nutritional needs and critically evaluated the pet food industry as it exists today. In this latest book, *Feeding Smart,* we go a few steps further and delve into the multitude of common myths and beliefs that exist about how to best feed dogs. As with all of The Science Dog books, this involves examining the scientific evidence that either supports *or* refutes these beliefs and exposing the myths whenever we find them. You will find no hyperbole, no outrageous claims, and no nutritional holy grail within these pages. Rather, you *will* encounter science-based evidence and nutritional facts. Some of this evidence may support your own personal beliefs about feeding dogs, and well, other evidence may not. Either way, be prepared to be informed with the latest data and science that is available regarding canine nutrition and feeding practices.

The book is divided into five parts. These are: Dogs, Nutrients, Ingredients, Foods, and Feeding. Each of the 38 chapters focuses on a commonly presented question that owners have about nutrition, dog foods, or feeding practices and then proceeds to review the most recent science on that topic. Because each chapter addresses a distinct question, the book's format allows readers to peruse the titles and select topics that are of greatest interest. In Part 1 (Dogs) you can learn about the correct nutritional classification of the domestic dog, *Canis familiaris* (*Is the dog a carnivore or an omnivore?*), whether or not dogs are capable of digesting starch, and how to determine if your dog is overweight. Other chapters take a look at what we currently know about dogs' scavenging behaviors (*Why do dogs eat poop?*) and how the microbes in our dogs' intestines help them to utilize nutrients and contribute to health.

Parts 2 and 3 dive into questions that dog owners frequently have about essential nutrients and about the ingredients that are found in dog foods. We take a look at the evidence regarding whether or not it is helpful to modify the fat in your dog's diet (*Do dogs need omega-3 fatty acids?*), if supplementing with a specific amino acid can influence behavior, and if there may be an excess of the mineral copper in some commercial pet foods. Dog foods today include a wide range of ingredients. These vary in terms of how they are processed (*What are protein meals and by-product meals?*), their original source, and how nutritious they may or may not be for dogs. There is also new information regarding the effects of cooking on the nutritional value of ingredients and comparing different sources of protein in foods. Finally, if you are interested in finding more environmentally friendly and sustainable foods for your dog, the chapters about plant source proteins and new research involving insect protein may capture your attention.

Part 4 (Foods) scrutinizes several common and highly successful marketing campaigns used by pet food companies to promote their products. These chapters help dog owners to sort fact from fiction regarding what a particular food can and cannot be expected to deliver in terms of their dog's health and wellness. This section also devotes five chapters to raw diets, which are increasingly popular and associated with a host of assertions and beliefs. Questions regarding health claims, food safety issues, and innovative approaches to producing different forms of raw foods for dogs are answered in these chapters. Part 4 concludes with examinations of human-grade foods and the effects of processing on the nutritional value of dog foods, topics that are of concern and interest to many owners and pet professionals. The final section, Part 5 (Feeding), includes new information about the history of feeding dogs, testing our dogs' food preferences, the benefits and limitations of food-delivery toys, and the nutrient value and safety of various types of chews and treats for dogs.

The five sections of *Feeding Smart* address many of the questions that dog owners have about selecting a healthful diet for their dogs. Because the focus of this book is on recently published and unbiased nutrition research, it is not intended to be an inclusive book in terms of covering all possible nutritional topics. However, because canine nutrition is a hotly debated topic and because researchers at universities around the world are studying dogs and dog foods (and publishing their results!), it is my hope that these 38 questions and the research that has been conducted to answer them will prove helpful.

Of course, academic research in not truly of value to dog owners unless we can gain some use from its results. To aid in this goal, each section of the book concludes with a chapter entitled, *The Science Dog Recommends*. These pages summarize the research and information presented in the preceding chapters and provide practical food selection and feeding tips for dog owners and pet professionals alike. These tips can also serve as a "go-to" section when you do not have the time for a deep-dive into the information presented regarding a particular topic or chapter.

Finally, considering the book's focus upon nutrition research and scientific evidence rather than personal opinion, one may ask if I, the author, ever venture to offer my own opinion on topics of nutrition and feeding. Well, yes, as a matter of fact, I do. Sometimes, as you will see, it is just too difficult to refrain from including my view about topics that I have personal and professional experience with and that I may hold strong opinions about. On other occasions I may include an opinion as a way to challenge current thinking, stimulate discussion, and well, just to shake things up a bit. To alert the reader to those instances when I am straying from the domain of science into the realm of opinion, the book includes this charming little fellow (who is also featured in other Science Dog books). When you see the soapbox, know that you are entering the realm of the author's opinion.

Up on my Soapbox

Whatever your own opinions and current practices about how to best feed our dogs are, the information presented in *Feeding Smart* should stimulate thought and discussion regarding the current science about who dogs are, what they need (and do not need) nutritionally, and how owners can critically assess foods and feeding practices to achieve a healthful approach to feeding their dogs. The ultimate goal of *Feeding Smart* is to encourage all who love dogs to seek out and critically review the evidence that science provides regarding beliefs and practices about nutrition and feeding. Doing so will aid you in developing your own informed opinions and in making the best possible, evidence-based decisions for your dog's diet and health.

Part 1 – Dogs

1. Is the dog a carnivore or an omnivore?

There continues to be a great deal of confusion (and opinion) regarding how to refer to the domestic dog, in terms of its classification and nutritional needs. Two primary camps exist. The first are those who identify the dog as a *carnivore* (meat-eating) animal. This group tends to focus on the predatory nature and food habits of the dog's closest cousin, the wolf. Conversely, the second camp are those inclined to classify the dog as an omnivore, a species that consumes *both* plants and meat. Followers in this group tend to focus on the dog's ability to consume and digest a wide variety of foods and the fact that dogs often scavenge different types of foods.

So, which is it? Is the domestic dog a carnivore or an omnivore?

Why the Confusion? From a scientific viewpoint, it appears that some of the confusion may arise from dual use of the term "carnivore". This term is used as both a taxonomic classification and as a description of a specie's feeding behavior and nutrient needs.

Let's first look at the dog's taxonomic classification. Both of our domesticated pets – the dog and the cat - are classified within the taxonomic order Carnivora. This order is large; it includes a diverse group of mammals representing over 280 species. The table on the following page compares the taxonomic classifications of the dog (*Canis familiaris*) and our other favorite animal companion, the cat (*Felis catus*).

TAXONOMY OF THE DOG AND CAT		
Taxonomic Group	Dog	Cat
Phyla	Animalia	Animalia
Class	Mammalia	Mammalia
Order	Carnivora	Carnivora
Family	Canidae	Felidae
Genus	*Canis*	*Felis*
Species	*familiaris*	*catus*

Some Eat Meat; Some Don't: While many of the species found in the Order Carnivora hunt and consume meat, not all are predatory or nutritionally carnivorous. Rather, species vary considerably in the degree of dependency that they have upon a meat-based diet and in their predatory behavior. For example, all the cat species, including the domestic cat, *Felis catus*, are obligate carnivores. In contrast, bears and raccoons consume both plant and animal foods, while the Giant Panda subsists on a vegetarian diet. Therefore, the nutrient needs and feeding behaviors of the animals classified within Carnivora exist along a broad spectrum, ranging from the obligate carnivores at one end to animals that are almost completely herbivorous at the other end. So, where does the domestic dog fall along this spectrum?

Cats vs. Dogs: We can examine this question by comparing our two best animal friends, the dog, and the cat. The cat is identified nutritionally as an "obligate carnivore" (sometimes called true carnivore). This title means that the cat is incapable of surviving on a vegetarian diet and must have at least some animal tissue

14

included in its diet. Put another way, a diet that is composed of all plant materials cannot meet all of a cat's essential nutrient needs. Specific nutrients that are problematic if Fluffy is fed a vegetarian diet include Vitamin A, a type of amino acid called taurine, and an essential fatty acid called arachidonic acid. All three of these nutrients are found in a form that cats can use in meat products but are not found in a usable form in plant foods. During evolution, cats either lost or never developed the ability to produce these nutrients from the precursor forms found in plant foods (see table below).

Essential Nutrient	Cat	Dog
Vitamin A	Requires source of preformed vitamin A*	Can convert beta-carotene from plants to Vitamin A
Arachidonic Acid (AA)	Required in diet, AA is an essential fatty acid*	Can produce enough AA to meet needs from Linoleic Acid
Taurine	High metabolic requirement; cannot use alternatives*	Lower metabolic need during most life stages; can use alternatives

* Nutrient is supplied only in animal tissues (meat)

The Adaptable Canine: In contrast, most of the canid species, including the domestic dog, are more generalist in their eating habits and subsequently in their nutrient needs. In the wild, wolves and coyotes exist as opportunistic predators, hunting and eating a variety of prey species. In addition to the flesh of their prey, wild canids readily consume viscera (stomach, intestines) which contain partially digested plant matter. Canid species also

15

scavenge carrion and garbage and regularly consume fruits, berries, mushrooms, and a variety of other plant materials.

Similar to its wild cousins, the domestic dog is a predatory species that also scavenges and is capable of obtaining nutrition from a wide variety of food types. During the process of domestication, as the dog gradually evolved from its ancestral wolf, dogs began to hunt less and scavenge more. This occurred as opportunities for scavenging increased alongside developing human communities and their associated food waste. Behavior changes that evolved at the same time included an enhanced tolerance of other dogs, reduced rigidity of social hierarchies, and reduced fear of human cohabitants. Although there is not complete agreement among experts, it is theorized that dogs that evolved more as scavengers were smaller and tamer than their wolf ancestors. It was this sub-population of dogs that eventually became fully domesticated and were selected for early forms of work with their human cohabitants.

Not only does the dog scavenge more and choose a wider variety of foods than does the cat (and probably more so also than wolves); the dog derives needed nutrients from plant foods more efficiently than cats. As reported in the previous table, dogs can use beta-carotene from plants as their source of vitamin A; they can produce enough arachidonic acid from its plant precursor, linoleic acid to meet their needs; and finally, although new research suggests that some dogs may need a dietary source of taurine in certain situations, dogs generally do not require a dietary source of taurine.

Last, anatomically, dogs' gastrointestinal tracts, from their mouths to their intestines, are consistent with other predatory species that consume a varied diet. Domestic dogs have some ability to grind food (molars), which is suggestive of an omnivorous diet. They possess a small intestine that is longer in length, relative to body size, than that of obligate carnivores, but shorter in length than that of herbivorous species. Metabolically, as we will see in the next chapter, dogs also possess an enhanced ability to digest plant starches when compared to their wolf ancestors.

The Evidence: When we look at the evidence, we see that both nutritionally and taxonomically, the dog is best classified as an omnivore or as some prefer, an opportunistic carnivore. What is known, regardless of what we call the dog, is that dogs can consume and derive nutrition from both animal and plant food sources. While it is true that the dog evolved from a species that made its living primarily through hunting and consuming prey, dogs also are adept scavengers who will consume a wide variety of food types, including both meats and plant foods. So, in the next chapter, let's take a deeper look at the dog's relationship with a specific class of plant foods – starches.

2. Can dogs digest plant starch (grains)?

One of the most contentiously defended viewpoints in recent years is that dogs should not be fed foods that contain digestible carbohydrate (starch).

Two primary arguments are used to defend this position. These are:

1. *Dogs are strict carnivores and have no dietary requirement for carbohydrate; and*

2. *Dogs are unable to efficiently digest starch. Therefore, including starch-providing ingredients in dog foods is unhealthy and provides no nutritional value.*

Like many persistent beliefs, there is both truth and falsehood to be found in these claims. Let's start with the first.

First Bit – Dogs are Strict Carnivores: As we now know, this belief is false. The term omnivore simply means that an animal consumes foods that are of animal and plant origin (dogs do this) and can derive essential nutrients from both animal and plant foods (ditto). Based upon this definition, animal nutritionists consider the dog to be an omnivore.

As we have discussed, the fact that dogs are omnivorous does not signify that they are not predatory (they are), nor that they do not seek out and enjoy eating meat (they do). All that it means is that dogs can consume and derive nutrients from both animal and plant matter.

Second Bit – Dogs Have No Requirement for Carbs: The second part of the statement is *true*. Dogs, like other animals, do not have a dietary requirement for carbohydrates. However, cooked starch provides a highly digestible energy source to dogs when included in their diet. There are two health-related benefits to this.

First, from a nutrition standpoint, dietary carbohydrate spares protein. This means that when a body uses carbohydrate to provide needed energy, dietary protein is conserved from being used for this purpose and continues to be available for use to provide essential amino acids, build and repair body tissues, and support a healthy immune system. Therefore, including at least some digestible carbohydrate in the diet of dogs is considered to be beneficial.

Second, dogs certainly can thrive on low-carbohydrate diets, provided such diets are balanced and contain all the essential nutrients. However, foods formulated in this way tend to be very energy dense (lots of calories packed into a small volume of food), primarily because they are high in fat. This can make it challenging to control portion size and to maintain proper body condition and weight in some dogs. In contrast, digestible starch provides less than half of the calories per unit weight compared to fat. Therefore, including at least some starch in a food can help to modulate food energy density and control portions and weight.

Can Dogs Digest Starch? The belief that dogs cannot digest starch is irrefutably *false*. Dogs can very efficiently digest cooked starch, just as humans do. Conversely, dogs cannot digest *raw* starch. Neither can we. This difference occurs because cooking causes expansion of the small granules that make up starch, changing its structure. This process, called gelatinization, allows an animal's digestive enzymes better access into the starch granules as they pass through the gastrointestinal tract, significantly enhancing digestibility. This difference between raw and cooked starch is true for humans as well as for dogs, and this fact explains why we generally do not munch on raw potatoes or enjoy corn on the cob without first roasting it.

Even more precisely, we know the degree to which cooking increases the digestibility of various starch sources in dogs. For example, ground grains such as rice, oats, and corn are only about 60 percent digestible when fed raw. Cooking these ingredients increases the dog's ability to digest them to almost 100 percent. Practically speaking, this means that if you feed your dog 100 grams of uncooked oats or rice, only 60 grams will make it into his body to nourish him; 40 grams ends up in the large intestine where microbes ferment some of it, and the remainder ends up in your yard, as feces. Conversely, when cooked, almost the entire 100 grams are digested and absorbed to nourish your dog.

Meet AMY2B: Compared to their wolf ancestors, dogs possess an enhanced ability to digest starch-containing ingredients, a change that is directly linked to domestication. In 2013, a ground-breaking paper by Swedish researcher Erik Axelsson identified a host of genetic changes that occurred as dogs evolved from ancestral wolves (1). Three of these changes were alterations of key genes that code for enzymes involved in starch digestion, most notably and consistently, one labeled AMY2B. This gene codes for the production of pancreatic amylase, an enzyme that functions to aid in the digestion of starch.

Although variation exists among individual dogs and breeds of differing geographic origin, the increased copies of the AMY2B gene correlate with higher levels of circulating pancreatic amylase in a dog's blood, which means that higher AMY2B leads to more efficient starch digestion (2,3,4). On average, dogs have a seven-fold higher copy number of this gene compared to present-day wolves. Interestingly, these changes in the dog's genetic makeup coincide with the expansion of human agricultural practices and increased reliance upon starch-providing plants in both human and dog diets.

A Few Answers: At this point in time, we know that dogs can better digest dietary starch compared to their wolf ancestors (and to present-day wolves). This enhanced ability is at least partially due to increased production of pancreatic amylase. We also know that, like us, dogs digest cooked starches very efficiently, but cannot utilize raw starch. We also know that the inclusion of at least some level of starch in a dog's diet provides an efficient source of energy (calories).

More Questions: Still, none of this information provides evidence for the healthfulness of a diet containing some starch versus a diet that contains low (or no) starch in terms of dog's vitality, ability to maintain a healthy body weight and condition, development of chronic health problems and longevity. Unfortunately, this has not stopped proponents of low carbohydrate or carbohydrate-free diets from making such claims.

What we need at this point, is evidence of whether or not dietary carbohydrate is harmful, beneficial or, neither. Dogs are generalists after all. It is quite possible (and I would argue probable) that they, like many animals, are capable of thriving on a wide variety of diet types, including those with varying amounts of (cooked) starch.

Cited Studies:

1. Axelsson E, Ratnakumar A, Arendt ML, et al. The genomic signature of dog domestication reveals adaptation to a starch-rich diet. *Nature* 2013; 495:360-364.

2. Arendt M, Fall, T, Lindblad-Toh K, Axelsson E. Amylase activity is associated with AMY2B copy numbers in dogs: Implications for dog domestication, diet, and diabetes. *Animal Genetics* 2014; 45:716-722.

3. Arendt M, Cairns KM, Ballard JWO, Savolainen P, Axelsson E. Diet adaptation in dogs reflects spread of prehistoric agriculture. *Heredity* 2016; 117:301-396.

4. Reiter T, Jagoda E, Capellini TD. Dietary variation and evolution of gene copy number among dog breeds. *PLOSOne* 2016; 11:e01148899.

3. What do dogs prefer to eat?

In the first two chapters, we learned that dogs are classified most correctly as omnivores and that they have evolved to efficiently digest cooked starch. Historically, as a species, dogs have obtained food through both predation and scavenging, consuming a variety of foods. However, we also know (at least anecdotally) that most dogs are highly attracted to meaty foods and flavors. For example, dog trainers use these preferences to select different levels of "treat value" for dogs. Almost invariably, the treats that are of highest value tend to be those that have a meaty texture, smell and taste.

Diet Selection Studies: It is a fact that domestic dogs are better adapted to scavenging and to a diet that is higher in starch-containing foods than were their wolf-like ancestors. However, just because dogs can consume and digest starch, it does not necessarily follow that a diet that contains a high proportion of digestible carbohydrate is the healthiest way to feed them. One way of approaching this question is to ask the dogs directly.

Historically, nutritionists have viewed diet selection in animals principally from the standpoint of energy balance. The basic assumption was that all animals, including dogs, eat to meet their energy (caloric) needs first. However, in recent years this premise has been challenged. There is evidence that a wide range of species, including many birds, fish, and mammals, will self-select diets containing consistent proportions of the three major macronutrients - protein, fat, and carbohydrate, and that they regulate and balance their nutrient intake to maximize lifespan and reproductive fitness. The recognition that macronutrient selection can be a driver for appropriate diet selection led to several research studies with dogs and cats. We can use this research to provide some practical answers regarding how best to feed our dogs.

What do Cats Choose? Domestic cats were studied first. The cats that were studied consistently selected diets that were high in protein and fat and low in carbohydrate (1). These results were not that surprising since cats are obligate carnivores and this profile was consistent with that of other obligate carnivores, including the cat's wild feline cousins. Interestingly, a second study found that domestic cats preferentially balanced their diets to a relatively rigid proportion of protein to fat, even when offered foods of different flavor preferences and containing either animal- or plant-based protein sources (2). Although flavor and smell were important influences, the strongest factor for food selection appeared to be the total amount of protein in the food, rather than its source.

What do Dogs Choose? To date, only two controlled studies of this nature have been completed with dogs. Similar to cats, dogs demonstrated a talent for self-selecting the macronutrient content of their diets (3,4). The studies were conducted by different research teams and used somewhat different methodologies, but both reported that dogs preferentially selected a diet that was low in carbohydrate, and high in fat and protein. When expressed as a percent of energy, dogs gravitated to a general distribution of 30 to 38 percent protein, 59 to 63 percent fat and only 3 to 7 percent carbohydrate. Interestingly, present-day wolves self-select diets that were even lower in carbohydrate - only about 1 percent.

It is also of note that initially the dogs in these studies were attracted to very high fat diets, but over a period of several days reduced the proportion of fat and moderately increase the proportion of protein. In addition, when dogs were allowed to choose these dietary proportions over a period of 10 days, they tended to over-consume calories. On average, the dogs gained almost 3.5 pounds in just 10 days of feeding. Because these were short-term feeding trials, we do not know if the dogs would have gradually calibrated their energy intake to better meet their daily needs or if they would have continued to gain weight. For feeding purposes, this is an important consideration.

How do Dogs Choose? Is it Smell or Taste? To answer this question, we turn to a series of clever studies that were conducted in India with free-ranging dogs. Free-ranging dogs exist in numerous areas of the world, including Mexico, Italy, Nepal, Japan, many African countries, and India. Some experts argue that these dogs are so numerous that they represent the most common way that dogs currently live, worldwide. Free-ranging dogs survive almost entirely by scavenging and occasionally augment their diet by hunting small animals.

A group of researchers who work regularly with free-ranging dogs in India became interested in finding out how exactly these dogs, with minimal human interference, select foods. They asked two questions: *Do dogs have a strong preference for meat in their diet?* and if so, *How do they select foods?*

Smell or Protein Content? In a series of cleverly designed studies the scientists offered 30 free-ranging adult dogs a variety of food choices (5). These foods were designed to disconnect the food components of meaty smells (using chicken broth-soaked bread) from the food's actual meat content (provided as kibble or cooked chicken). Here is what they discovered:

🐾 *Meat smell over carbs*: The dogs consistently chose bread soaked in chicken broth over dry bread or bread soaked in water, even though chicken broth contains a very small amount of protein. When allowed to choose visually (not by smell), the dogs selected chicken meat first over chicken-soaked bread or dry bread.

🐾 *Smell beats all*: When the dogs were offered kibble (high protein food) or bread (low protein food) soaked with varying concentrations of chicken broth, the dogs chose according to *smell*, not in accordance with the actual amount of meat present in the food.

🐾 *A doggy "Rule of Thumb"*: The cumulative results of the experiments support the existence of the following rule of thumb for food choice: *"Choose the food that smells the most intensely of meat first."* This means that the dogs preferred foods that smelled of meat (but that were not necessarily good sources of protein) over those that smelled less meaty, even when the less meaty smelling foods contained more meat ingredients and had a higher protein content. This of course, makes sense, since in nature, a stronger meat smell is highly correlated with high meat and protein content and invariably predicts higher meat quantity. This relationship only becomes skewed when clever experimenters enter the picture and mess with it.

The authors concluded that while domestic free-ranging dogs have clearly adapted a scavenging lifestyle, they appear to have done so without relinquishing a strong preference for meat. They suggested that while the domestic dog has indeed evolved to digest carbohydrate more efficiently and to exist on a carbohydrate-rich scavenged diet, dogs continue to be strongly attracted to the smell of meat and will preferentially select meat-smelling foods.

Take Away for Dog Folks: So, what do these research studies tell us about feeding our own dogs? Well, we have learned that when given a choice, dogs preferentially select a diet that is high in protein and fat and low in starch. We also have some evidence that the selection of foods is strongly influenced by smell, in particular the smell of meat, but that the actual proportion of meat in the food may be less influential on dogs' choice. For dog trainers, this means that a meaty-smelling treat may have very high training value simply because of its smell, rather than because of the level of actual meat that it contains.

Finally, we know from the previous chapter that dogs can better digest starch in their diet compared to their wolf ancestors. This increased capability is at least partially due to increased production of pancreatic amylase. We also know that the inclusion of at least some level of starch in a dog's diet provides an efficient source of energy (calories).

Regardless, the fact that dogs gravitate to a diet that is high in protein and fat and low in starch should not be confused with evidence that such a diet has been proven to be healthier or is capable of preventing illness. We must remember that preference does not necessarily translate into healthfulness – this is supported by the fact that dogs who were allowed to self-select rapidly gained weight when they consumed a diet that was high in fat and protein.

Cited Studies:

1. Hewson-Hughes AK, Hewson-Hughes VL, Miller AT, et al. Geometric analysis of macronutrient selection in the adult domestic cat, *Felis catus. Journal of Experimental Biology* 2011; 214:1039-1051.

2. Hewson-Hughes AK, Colyer A, Simpson SJ, Raubenheimer D. Balancing macronutrient intake in a mammalian carnivore: disentangling the influences of flavor and nutrition. *Royal Society of Open Science* 2016; 3:160081.

3. Hewson-Hughes AK, Hewson-Hughes VL, Colyer A, et al. Geometric analysis of macronutrient selection in breeds of the domestic dog, *Canis familiaris. Behavioral Ecology* 2013; 24:293-304.

4. Roberts MT, Bermingham EN, Cave NJ, Young W, McKenzie CM, Thomas DG. Macronutrient intake of dogs, self-selecting diets varying in composition offered ad libitum. *Journal of Animal Physiology and Nutrition* 2018; 102:568-575.

5. Bhadra A, Bhattacharjee D, Paul M and Ghadra A. The meat of the matter: A thumb rule for scavenging dogs. *Ethology, Ecology and Evolution* 2016; 28:427-440.

4. *Why do dogs eat poop (coprophagize)?*

Poop eating – Lots of dogs do it. They seem to enjoy it. Owners, on the other hand, not so much. Most would like to understand this habit and stop or prevent it, if possible.

The technical term for poop-eating, of any type, is coprophagy. Many dogs readily consume the feces of other animal species – rabbit, deer, horse, opossum, and raccoon. Additionally, dogs who share their home with a cat often find poop of the feline variety to be especially tasty. A somewhat smaller proportion of dogs consume the excrement of other *dogs*. This is called *conspecific coprophagy*. It is these dogs that we are focusing on in this chapter.

Conspecific Coprophagy (Dogs Eating Dog Poop)

Believe it or not, there is science available about this topic – a few actual studies, even. Let's review what we currently know about dogs who eat canine feces, why they may do this, and how to best prevent or manage this unsavory behavior.

It's Normal in Moms: Coprophagy is considered to be a normal behavior in mother dogs. For the first several weeks after her pups are born, the mother ingests all of her pups' feces. She does this for hygiene purposes to keep her puppies and the whelping area clean, and also because the associated licking and cleaning of the puppy provides needed stimulation for elimination. Mothers typically stop this after 2 to 3 weeks, once their puppies are beginning to walk and can urinate and defecate without aid.

It's Common: Stool eating is not only observed in mothers with young puppies, however. It is also relatively common in adult dogs. For example, a 2018 survey study asked dog owners a series of questions regarding conspecific coprophagy (1). The researchers received almost 1500 responses. (Clearly, this was something dog owners wanted to get off of their chests). The results showed that between **16 and 23%** of dogs either occasionally or frequently consumed the feces of other dogs. The dogs who frequently consumed canine feces were more likely to live in multiple dog homes than dogs who did not coprophagize (more about this later). Results also showed that in addition to being a commonly reported behavior, the majority of poop-eating dogs (82 %) directed their attention to feces that were fresh – no more than two days old. This of course, was additionally unpleasant for the dogs' owners.

For the researchers however, this latter fact was significant. Most intestinal parasites need to remain in the environment for several days or longer before becoming infective. This fact suggests that coprophagy has been selected for during the dog's evolutionary history. Rapid consumption of recently voided feces would reduce the risk of infection with intestinal parasites. The researchers suggested that this tendency provides support for the "*poop eating is a normal dog behavior*" theory.

Finally, evidence from this study dispelled several prevalent myths. Coprophagy was *not* associated with a dog's sex, neuter status or age. Nor were early weaning, late or difficult housetraining, or compulsive-like behavior problems associated with a dog's chance of developing a poop-eating habit. Most important for our interests, this study, and others, dispelled one of the most prevalent myths about poop eating – a dog's diet.

Diet and Poop Eating: Despite the many diet/nutrient-related beliefs about coprophagy in dogs, there is no scientific evidence that suggests dogs consume feces because of a particular nutrient deficiency or because they are fed a specific type of food. So, when someone tells you that your dog consumes poop because: (a) you feed a certain brand of dog food; (b) you feed a food with too much carbohydrate; (c) you feed a food with too little carbohydrate; or (d) your dog is expressing a deficiency in [pick a nutrient that is easy to pronounce], feel free to tell that person that he is full of...... dog poop. No studies to date have found an association between dogs' diets and their propensity to develop coprophagy.

There is one diet-related *behavior* that correlates with coprophagy, however. Dogs who are reportedly "greedy" or rapid eaters are more likely to also enjoy eating feces. This observation suggests that dogs who experience higher levels of hunger may be more inclined to coprophagize. However, a pair of studies that tracked behavior in a group of dogs that initially had food available at all times and were switched to restricted meal feeding reported no difference in stool eating when the dogs were fed less food (2,3). This suggests that hunger may not be an underlying cause of the greedy eater connection.

Wait. You Can Eat That? As mentioned previously, the survey study found that dogs who frequently consume the feces of other dogs were more likely to live in a multiple dog home. Of course, this might simply reflect increased opportunity (i.e., more poop equals more poop eating). A second set of researchers took a deeper look at this connection (4). They conducted in-person and written interviews with the owners of 70 dogs; 30 dogs were identified as conspecific coprophagizers and 40 dogs refrained from eating feces.

Similar to the larger survey study, no associations were found between coprophagy and a dog's sex, reproductive status, living situation or type or diet. However, poop eating was significantly *more* likely in homes that not only had another dog but had another dog who also engaged in coprophagy. This should really not be surprising, given what we now understand about observational learning in dogs (they are very good at it). Dogs not only follow the attention of other dogs and will investigate items their friends are interested in; they also are capable of learning new behaviors from each other through observation. It seems that coprophagy may be readily learned from housemates. (Friends don't let friends eat poop alone).

On a personal level, I rather suspected this. Our very first Golden, Fauna, was an intermittent poop eater. She apparently introduced this habit to one of her younger sisters, Roxie. Roxie then passed it along to Sparks, who gladly handed the torch over to Gusto, who mentored Cadie.......and onward. Today, we have Alice, who offers tutoring services to anyone who is interested. Lucky for us, neither Cooper nor Stanley have yet to take her up on this generous offer.

Can Coprophagy be Prevented? It is now clear that a substantial number of healthy adult dogs indulge in the occasional poop treat. The general consensus is that coprophagy is a normal canine behavior, not an aberration. Its functional history is probably related to hygiene, parasite prevention, and possibly to scavenging behavior. This does not mean that owners of poop-eaters must accept this or allow it to continue. Rather, it means that there are probably no underlying health or behavioral issues in dogs who coprophagize and that it should be treated as a normal behavior that can be modified through management (mostly) and behavior modification (somewhat).

Before we look at what can help, let's review what the science currently tells us does NOT work.

Unsuccessful Remedies:

🐾 *Commercial supplements*: There are a lot of these. They contain a lot of things. Some claim to either change the taste of feces or alter fecal odor. Others profess to contain nutrients that are lacking in the dog's diet and that, once provided will magically stop the poop-eating. *None* of these products provide controlled studies demonstrating efficacy. Owners who try these products report a reduction in poop-eating in *less than 2 percent of cases*. Save your pennies.

🐾 *Reducing carbs*: This is a popular one. Although an early study suggested that a high carbohydrate diet may increase a dog's tendency to eat stools, there is no research evidence to date showing that reducing carbohydrate in a food reduces coprophagy in dogs. Yeesh. Carbs get blamed for everything these days.

🐾 *Reducing boredom*: Well, this is always a good thing to do, of course. Increasing play, exercise, and opportunities for owner interactions are *all* good things for our dogs. However, the only data that are available show that providing different types of toys to kenneled dogs as an attempt to relieve boredom did not reduce coprophagy. But really, do all of this stuff with your dog anyway.

🐾 *Punishment:* In the large survey study, some owners used an electronic collar or other aversive in an attempt to punish coprophagy. Similar to the use of supplements, attempting to punish coprophagy had an abysmal success rate – less than 2 percent. Please, do not do this. It does not work, and it is not a nice thing to do to your dog.

Take Away for Dog Folks: There are several important points to take away from these recent research studies and the evidence that they provide:

🐾 *Coprophagy is a normal dog behavior,* exhibited by many healthy adult dogs, in different living situations that are fed a wide variety of foods. Some dogs eat poop. We need to accept this and move on.

🐾 *Dogs pay attention to what their friends are eating.* If you have a dog who eats poop, it is likely you will have more. Sorry.

🐾 *Poop eating is resistant to change.* Diet supplements do not work. Punishment does not work and is a bad thing to do anyway.

🐾 *What can you do?* Pick up your yard frequently. Supervise your dog. Reduce or completely prevent access to feces. Train a solid "Leave it" response using reward-based methods. This means that your dog learns that you consistently have a yummy treat that is much more attractive to her than the poop she is considering consuming (com'on now, it's not a high bar to clear).

🐾 **Enjoy your dog.** Spend time, have fun together. Train that "Leave it" and chill a bit. Yeah, he might eat poop. But then, you probably do a few things that your dog finds annoying too.

Cited Studies:

1. Hart B, Hart L, Thigpen AP, Tran A, Bain M. The paradox of canine conspecific coprophagy. *Veterinary Medicine and Science* 2018; 4:106-114.

2. Crowell-Davis SL, Barry K, Ballam JM, Laflamme DP. The effect of caloric restriction on the behavior of pen-housed dogs: Transition from unrestricted to restricted diet. *Applied Animal Behavior Science* 1995; 43:27-41.

3. Crowell-Davis SL, Barry K, Ballam JM, Laflamme DP. The effect of caloric restriction on the behavior of pen-housed dogs: Transition from restriction to maintenance diets and long-term effects. *Applied Animal Behavior Science* 1995; 43:43-61.

4. Amaral AR, Porsani MY, Martins PO, Teixeira FA, et al. Canine coprophagic behavior is influenced by coprophagic cohabitant. *Journal of Veterinary Behavior* 2018; 28:35-39.

5. *Why do some dogs gain weight so easily?*

The Labs have a problem.

Actually, *some* Labs have a problem. They are fat.

However, it may not be their fault (or their owners' fault) ...

It's in Their Genes: A few years ago, a group of researchers at the University of Cambridge in the UK discovered a genetic anomaly in a small group of overweight Labrador Retrievers (1). Specifically, this genetic modification is a short deletion sequence in a gene called *POMC*. The presence of this deletion was found to be positively associated with both a tendency to overeat and an increased risk of obesity. Technically then, because the problem is a *deletion* issue, this is not so much a "fat gene" as it is the *lack* of a body weight control gene. (Because it is catchy though inaccurate, the former description took off in social media).

In the study, researchers examined all possible genetic sequences that were candidates for a "fat gene" The *POMC* deletion was found in 10 of 15 overweight dogs and in only 2 of 18 lean dogs. Curiosity piqued, the investigators went on to test dogs from 39 other breeds and did not find the mutation. The only other breed that was found to carry the gene deletion sequence was the Flat Coated Retriever (FCR). Although FCRs are not typically associated with obesity, when the researchers tested a group of 200 FCRs, they found that, just as in the Labradors, the mutant *POMC* gene was positively associated with higher body weight and greater food motivation.

Confirming Evidence: As we always like to see with good science, these results were subsequently corroborated by a separate and unrelated team of researchers (2). Similar to the earlier work, they found the mutation only in Labs and not in other breeds. One difference was that this second set of results suggests that the *POMC* deletion variant may be inherited as a simple recessive gene rather than as having an additive effect, as proposed by the researchers in the initial study.

It now appears that some (not all) Labs do indeed lack a body weight control gene that makes them more susceptible to overweight conditions and to being highly motivated to overeat. Based upon even more recent evidence, it is quite possible that we will begin to see this "fat gene" and other genetic mutations that predispose dogs to being overweight in other breeds as well (3).

Regardless, this information can be helpful for owners who have a difficult time keeping their happy and energetic (and food-loving) dog from packing on the pounds. (See *The Science Dog Recommends* at the end of this Section).

Cited Studies:

1. Raffan E, Dennis RJ, O'Donovan, et al. A deletion in the canine *POMC* gene is associated with weight and appetite in obesity-prone Lab. Retriever dogs. *Cell Metabolism* 2016; 23: 893-900.

2. Mankowska M, Krzeminska P, Graczyk M, Switonski M. Confirmation that a deletion in the *POMC* gene is associated with body weight in Labrador Retriever dogs. *Research in Veterinary Science* 2017; 112:116-118.

3. The genetic basis of obesity and related metabolic diseases in humans and companion animals. *Genes* 2020; 11:1378. doi: 10.3390/genes11111378.

6. Is MY dog too fat?

Although there may be a genetic predisposition for overweight conditions in some (probably a small number of) dogs, it is undisputable that *many* dogs who live as pets in homes are overweight. Breed and the lack of a body weight control gene cannot be singularly responsible for these numbers.

A Few Statistics:

🐾 Obesity continues to be the *number one* nutritional problem in pet dogs in the United States.

🐾 According to the Association of Pet Obesity Prevention (APOP), surveyed veterinarians classified *53 percent* of their canine patients as either overweight or obese.

🐾 In the same survey, only *22 percent* of the owners identified their dog as being overweight.

Why the Disconnect? A common theory used to explain this mismatch between what owners perceive and what their dog actually looks like is that owners simply have not been taught how to recognize overweight conditions in dogs. This theory posits that many owners lack the ability to differentiate between a dog who is at ideal weight versus one who is overweight.

In an attempt to provide this type of education to owners, pet food companies have created Body Condition Scores. These are standardized five to 9-point visual scales designed to help owners and veterinarians correctly assess a dog's weight and body condition.

On the following page is a generic example of a five-point BCS scale (you have probably seen these hanging in your veterinarian's office):

Dog Body Condition Chart

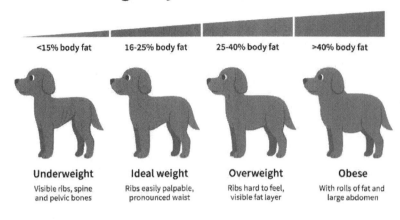

<15% body fat	16-25% body fat	25-40% body fat	>40% body fat
Underweight	**Ideal weight**	**Overweight**	**Obese**
Visible ribs, spine and pelvic bones	Ribs easily palpable, pronounced waist	Ribs hard to feel, visible fat layer	With rolls of fat and large abdomen

Problem Solved? Well, unfortunately, these visual aids have been around for more than 20 years, and our dogs are still fat. Perhaps the scales are not being used? Are they difficult to understand or interpret?

To find out, a group of researchers asked the question: "*If we give dog owners a BCS tool, show them how to use it, and then ask them to evaluate their own dog using the tool, will their assessments improve?*" Their hypothesis was optimistic. They believed this would do the trick. (Spoiler alert – They were wrong).

The Study: This was a pre-test/post-test study design that included a group of 110 owners and their dogs (1). In the pre-test phase, owners were asked to assess their dog's body condition. No guidance was provided, and the owner was required to select one word that best described their dog from a set of five terms. These were: *very thin, thin, ideal weight, overweight, or markedly obese*. Following this part of the study, the owners were provided with a five-point BCS chart that used the same five descriptors along with visual silhouettes and short descriptions. They were given instructions of how to use the chart and were instructed to assess their dog a second time. The investigating veterinarian also assessed the dogs using the BCS chart and a physical examination.

Results: Prior to using the BCS chart, a majority of the owners (66 %) incorrectly assessed their dog's body condition. Most owners dramatically underestimated their dog's body condition, believing their overweight dog to be at or near his or her ideal weight. These results are consistent with those reported by other researchers and with the APOP survey.

What is truly surprising is that, in the second phase of the study, after being taught to use the BCS chart, these misperceptions persisted, showing virtually no change; 65 % of the owners were incorrect and only 15 % changed their original score (some up/some down, and some from correct to incorrect!). The majority of owners continued to see their plump dog as being at his or her optimal weight.

Here is where things get really weird.

When queried, most owners (77 %) stated that they believed that using the BCS chart had significantly improved their ability to estimate their dog's body condition (huh?). This statement was made despite the fact that few owners had changed their scores after they learned to use the chart. Moreover, those who said that the chart had helped them fared no better in post-test success than the those who believed that the chart did not help them.

Take Away for Dog Folks: This study confirms what several other researchers have reported and what the APOP statistics tell us; dog owners tend to underestimate their dog's weight and body condition, seeing a dog who is overweight as ideal. It also provides an additional bit of important information. Even when owners are shown how to identify an overweight dog, they continue to be unable to correctly assess their own dog.

We still get it wrong. Why is this happening? There are a few possible reasons:

🐾 ***Fido is not fat; he just has big bones***: Resistance to seeing one's own dog as overweight may be a form of denial, similar to the well-documented misperception that many parents have regarding their child's weight. Because being over-weight is viewed negatively by others, is associated with well-known health risks, and may be perceived as reflecting badly upon an owner's ability to care properly for their dog, denial may be quite an attractive alternative to the truth.

🐾 ***Confirmation bias***: In this pre-test/post-test situation, peo-ple may have resisted changing their scores following train-ing simply because, well, people hate to be proven wrong. If an owner had preconceived beliefs about his dog's weight and initially assigned a moderate score, he might subse-quently (and unconsciously) use the BCS chart to confirm that belief, however misguided it was.

🐾 ***Food is love***: Other studies of owners and dogs have reported that a substantial number of owners admit that they are un-willing to deny food to their dog, even when they know their dog is overweight, because they view feeding as an important outlet for love and nurturing (2). Similarly, owners tend to resist changing established feeding habits with their dogs even when aware of the adverse health effects to their dogs of being overweight (3).

The results of this study suggest that we have a way to go re-garding our ability to recognize and prevent overweight condi-tions in our own dogs. If you are wondering if you have correctly assessed your dog's body weight and condition, take a few minutes, review a BCS chart and keep on your skeptical specta-cles as you assign your dog a score.

If you are a trainer, doggy day care owner, groomer, veterinarian, veterinary technician, or other pet professional who works daily with dog owners, post a BCS chart in your facility, have a weight scale handy, and ask your clients to regularly weigh and assess their dogs. Help owners to keep their dogs slender and in proper body condition. Provide guidelines to help dogs to trim down, encourage exercise, training, and play activities. Help owners to understand that keeping a dog trim is one of the best ways that we can support their health and demonstrate our love for them.

Cited Studies:

1. Eastland-Jones RC, German AJ, Holden SL, Biourge V, Pickavance LC. Owner misperception of canine body condition persists despite use of a body condition score chart. *Journal of Nutritional Science* 2014; 3:e45;1-5.

2. Kienzle E, Bergler R, Mandernach A. A comparison of the feeding behavior and the human-animal relationship in owners of normal and obese dogs. *Journal of Nutrition* 1998; 128:2779S-2782S.

3. Bland IM, Guthrie-Jones A, Taylor RD. Dog obesity: Owner attitudes and behavior. *Preventive Veterinary Medicine* 2009; 92:333-340.

7. What is the gut microbiome & how does nutrition influence it?

The dog's gut microbiome and its impact on health and disease have received a great deal of study in recent years. However, many dog owners are not quite sure what this term refers to, what the microbiome does, and how the food that they feed to their dog may influence their dog's gut microbiome and health.

What is the Gut Microbiome? The gut microbiome, more correctly referred to as the intestinal microbiome, is comprised of all of the microorganisms (primarily bacteria) that live within your dog's intestinal tract. When counting from the mouth to the end of the large intestine, there are literally *trillions* of cells involved. By any measure, this is a whole lot of bugs.

The relationship between these organisms and the host animal (in this case, your dog) is *symbiotic* or mutually beneficial. A healthy dog and his bugs coexist nicely, with both deriving benefits from their living arrangement. The dog provides a warm place to live, plenty of food, and the company of other bugs. In return, the gut microbes have numerous functions that benefit the dog. They break down (ferment) certain food components and produce a host of beneficial nutrients and other end products, called *postbiotics*. These compounds nourish cells lining the intestine and, when absorbed, influence the dog's nutritional status, health, and possibly even behavior. Here are a few specific examples:

🐾 *Immune system*: Bacterial populations function to "educate" a dog's immune system regarding discrimination between harmless/helpful bacteria and potentially pathogenic, disease-causing microbes.

🐾 *Short-chain fatty acids:* Certain species of bacteria produce compounds called short-chain fatty acids (SCFAs) as end products. These compounds moderate the pH of the intestinal environment, have a role in satiety (feeling full after a meal) and provide an important energy source to cells lining the dog's intestine, among other benefits.

🐾 *Serotonin:* More than *80 percent* of the body's serotonin, an important neurotransmitter, is produced from the amino acid tryptophan by intestinal microbes (yeah, wow!). This discovery was the impetus for the relatively new theory of the gut-brain axis and its effects upon behavior, which is a booming field of scientific inquiry.

🐾 *Vitamin K:* Intestinal microbes provide most, if not all, of a dog's Vitamin K requirement. Although there is not consensus, there is evidence that healthy dogs do not have a dietary requirement for this vitamin, as their needs can be completely provided by gut microbes.

What Bugs? In all animals, including dogs, the concentrations of microbes and predominant bacterial species differ depending on the part of the intestinal tract that you are looking at. For example, a completely distinct set of bugs inhabit a dog's mouth compared to what you find in the same dog's large intestine. Generally speaking, the microbes that we are most interested in and that are important in terms of health benefits are those located in the large intestine. Most of these bacterial species come from five taxonomic phyla that are common to the microbiome of all dogs. Three of these, Fusobacterium, Bacteroides and Firmicutes, make up the largest proportion of fecal microbes. It is important to note that a phylum is a pretty darn large group of bugs. For example, Firmicutes, the largest phylum of bacteria, includes over 200 different genera, and species that number in the thousands. That is a lot of bacterial diversity, no doubt! The table on the following page provides just one example.

Nomenclature	Example
Phylum	Firmicutes
Class	Bacilli
Order	Lactobacillales
Family	Lactobacillaceae
Genus	*Lactobacillus*
Species	*Lactobacillus acidophilus*

Lactobacillus acidophilus
One species within the Firmicutes phylum

When dogs become ill, especially in the case of chronic gastrointestinal disorders, significant changes can occur in both the species and the numbers of microbes that make up the gut microbiome. For our purposes, we will examine the gut microbiome of *healthy* dogs and take a look at what we currently understand about how what we feed dogs influences the make-up of their gut microbiome.

Feeding the Gut (Microbiome): Foods that are well digested are broken down largely in the small intestine. The resulting nutrients are absorbed and provide essential functions in the body. Any undigested or partially digested food travels on to the large intestine where it provides food for gut microbes. The composition of these undigested food stuffs – protein, fat, carbs, fiber – play a significant role in determining the types of bugs that proliferate and dominate in an individual dog's large intestine. Ultimately, the numbers of these bugs and their end products influence the dog's health and wellness.

What dietary factors are important to consider?

Protein vs. Carbohydrates/Fiber: Simply changing the proportion of protein or carbohydrate in a dog's diet can lead to rapid changes in the composition of gut microbes in the dog's intestines. Increases in plant carbohydrates and fiber lead to an increase in Firmicutes genera, several of which are classified as fiber fermenters. This means that these species are associated with the fermentation of dietary fiber and increased production of short-chain fatty acids. One of these SCFAs is a compound called butyrate, which is an important source of energy for cells lining the dog's intestine. The use of prebiotics is an approach to increasing these microbes and their production of beneficial SCFAs.

Conversely, when dogs are fed a high protein, low carbohydrate diet, Firmicutes bugs decrease in number while other bacterial species increase. The increases are usually in the Proteobacteria and Fusobacteria genera and include species that are important for the fermentation of protein. Interestingly, it appears that the source of the protein in the food is less important than is protein level. Both plant-source and animal-source food proteins will have this effect on gut microbes.

Cooked vs. Raw Diet: Several studies have examined changes to dogs' microbiome when dogs were switched from an extruded dry (kibble) food to a raw meat diet. In all cases, feeding dogs a raw food was associated with modified bacterial populations and in some cases, with an increase in both total numbers and microbial diversity. However, because the raw diets were consistently higher in protein and fat and lower in carbohydrate, it is not known if the changes were due principally to macronutrient differences (higher protein), processing differences (raw), or a combination of these factors. It is important to note here that an increase in microbial number is not necessarily a benefit. There is also evidence that some dogs fed raw foods have higher levels of pathogenic microbes in their feces and may be at increased risk of infection (this is discussed in detail in Section 4).

Protein Quality: This is an important one. Protein quality is determined by a protein source's amino acid composition and its digestibility. Feeding a high-quality protein source at optimal levels results in minimal amounts of undigested protein entering the large intestine. Conversely, when dogs are fed poor quality protein, a relatively larger proportion of undigested protein ends up in the large intestine. Certain species of bacteria there are happy to see this protein and rapidly digest it – a process aptly called *putrefaction*. Some of the end products of microbial putrefaction are considered to be undesirable and potentially harmful to dogs' health. These are implicated in a number of chronic inflammatory disorders such as atopy (topical allergies), renal disease, and several forms of gastrointestinal disease. To minimize these effects, one of the most important dietary goals when feeding our dogs, regardless of the type of food that is fed, is to provide an optimal level of high-quality protein.

Prebiotics: The term prebiotic refers to selectively fermented food ingredients that provide nutrients to beneficial intestinal bacteria while *not* feeding the less desirable bacterial species and potential pathogens. Prebiotics are either incorporated directly into a dog food or provided as a nutritional supplement, sometimes in combination with a probiotic.

Most prebiotics are types of fiber or resistant starches that are moderately to highly fermentable by gut microbes. Examples are fructooligosaccharides (FOS), beet pulp, potato fiber, and inulin, among others. Because they are indigestible (i.e., cannot be broken down by the dog's digestive enzymes), prebiotics bypass most of the small intestine and end up in the large intestine, where they are fermented to varying degrees by gut microbes. The expected health benefits of prebiotics arise from two things:

48

🐾 *End products of fermentation*: Intestinal microbes ferment the prebiotic as a source of energy and subsequently produce SCFAs. These compounds provide the benefits that were discussed previously.

🐾 *Promotion of "good bugs"*: There is some evidence (but not very much) that feeding prebiotics can increase the numbers of desirable bacterial species in dogs. However, these beneficial alterations are influenced not only by the mixture of fibers that are fed, but also by the diet's underlying carbohydrate and protein levels and by a dog's baseline microbial populations. Additionally, and importantly, a rather thin line exists between feeding levels of prebiotic fibers that provide benefit versus a higher level that leads to loose stools and diarrhea (oops). Ultimately, while there may be some benefit to prebiotics, the current evidence does not support their universal use as an approach to improving the makeup of the gut microbiome.

Probiotics: While prebiotics are compounds intended to *feed* a dog's microbiome, probiotics are the bugs themselves. These are typically formulations of live organisms delivered in amounts that are intended to alter the dog's gut microbiome in a beneficial way. The two most commonly used microbes are species of *Bifidobacteria* and *Lactobacillus*, although several others have been studied. Most of the studies of probiotic use with dogs have targeted dogs with gastrointestinal diseases such as acute gastroenteritis (i.e., garbage gut or stress diarrhea) or more serious disorders such as inflammatory bowel disease or protein-losing enteropathy. While there is some research suggesting possible benefits to ill dogs, there are no data that suggest health benefits of probiotics when provided to healthy dogs.

Take Away for Dog Folks: The relationship between dogs and their gut microbiome is mutually beneficial. A healthy dog provides a great environment for a wide variety of microorganisms.

The bugs, in turn, produce a variety of postbiotics and support health and wellness. A win-win for both.

Dietary factors that significantly influence the make-up of a dog's gut microbiome include the amount and type of starch and fiber, the level and quality of protein, and whether the food is cooked (extruded) versus raw. A special call out to protein quality – *pay attention to it.*

Prebiotics, which are types of fiber that some microbes ferment, can lead to an increase in postbiotics that are associated with health in dogs. However, feeding the correct type of prebiotic, in what type of diet matrix, and at effective levels, remains rather elusive. The bottom line – if your dog is healthy, he probably does not need a prebiotic. Ditto on probiotics. While there are some studies showing benefits for dogs with certain forms of GI disease, there are little data to support the use of a probiotic with a healthy dog.

Cited Studies:

1. Barko PC, McMichael MA, Swanson KS, Williams DA. The gastrointestinal microbiome: A review. *Journal of Veterinary Internal Medicine* 2018; 32:9-25.

2. Pilla R, Suchodolski JS. The gut microbiome of dogs and cats, and the influence of diet. *Veterinary Clinics of North America: Small Animal Practice* 2021; 51:605-621.

3. Wernimont SM, Radosevich J, Jackson MI, Ephraim E, Badri DV, MacLeay JM, Jewell DE, Suchodolski JS. The effects of nutrition on the gastrointestinal microbiome of cats and dogs: Impact on health and disease. *Frontiers in Microbiology* 2020; doi:10.3389/fmicb.2020.01266.

DOGS - The Science Dog Recommends

Here are a few practical tips, knowing what we do about the evolutionary history and nutrient needs of the domestic dog, *Canis familiaris*:

- Dogs share a predatory history with their closest cousin, the wolf. Behaviorally, we see this history in the form of strong chase, grab and shake behaviors when dogs are playing (or, if unsupervised and allowed to actually hunt small animals).

- Dogs also scavenge and consume a wide variety of food types, including starch-containing foods. These behaviors take the form of investigating and eating all sorts of unpalatable items. Garbage robbing, counter-crawling, and coprophagy (poop eating) are also forms of scavenging behaviors.

- Dogs, like humans, can efficiently digest and utilize cooked starch in foods. Also, like humans, dogs *do not* efficiently digest uncooked plant starch. Including cooked starch sources in a dog's diet provides available energy and spares dietary protein from being used to provide energy.

- Technically, dogs are classified as omnivores. However, they are omnivores that prefer meat and preferentially select meaty foods. When provided with a choice, dogs self-select a diet that is high in protein and fat and low in carbohydrate.

- There is no evidence that dogs who coprophagize have underlying health or behavioral problems. Rather, coprophagy should be viewed as a normal (but unsavory) canine behavior that can be modified through management practices and reward-based behavior modification techniques.

🐾 A healthy gut microbiome is important and necessary for your dog's health. Support it by feeding foods that are digestible, contain high quality protein, and include at least some dietary carbohydrate and fiber.

🐾 Multiple factors, one of which is genetics, influence the high prevalence of overweight conditions in dogs. Provide your dog with plenty of enjoyable and stimulating exercise, and feed optimal amounts of food to keep your dog trim and well-muscled. Weigh your dog regularly and use a standard BCS chart to carefully monitor your dog's weight and body condition throughout life.

Part 2 – Nutrients

8. Do dogs need omega-3 fatty acids?

The omega-3 family of fatty acids receives quite a bit of attention these days, and with good reason. We have known for some time that increasing omega-3 fatty acids and improving the ratio of omega-6 to omega-3 fats in a dog's diet are associated with certain health benefits. Although the effects of adding these fats to foods are often overstated, it is probable that ensuring optimal levels of omega-3 fatty acids in dogs' foods is a healthful dietary change to make. So, what do dog owners need to know about these nutrients?

Omega-6 and Omega-3 Fatty Acids: Dietary fatty acids are classified into groups called families. Two families that are important nutritionally are the omega-6 fatty acids and the omega-3 fatty acids. Both types are important, but our present-day dog foods (like human foods) tend to contain an over-abundance of omega-6 fatty acids. This occurs as a result of the types of ingredients and foods produced by modern-day agricultural systems. Western food crops are high in linoleic acid (LA), the parent omega-6 fatty acid, and relatively low in alpha-linolenic acid (ALA), the parent omega-3 fatty acid.

The predominance of omega-6 fatty acids in the plant foods that we produce has repercussions throughout the food chain. It is only in recent years that the importance of balancing omega-6 and omega-3 fatty acids in foods has become evident. For dogs, as for humans, this translates into approaches that increase dietary omega-3 fatty acids and in some cases, simultaneously decrease omega-6 fatty acids.

Which Omega-3s are Important? There are three omega-3 fatty acids that you should pay attention to. These are the parent fatty acid alpha-linolenic acid and two of its long-chain derivatives, eicosapentaenoic acid (EPA) and docosahexaenoic acid (DHA). It is these two latter fatty acids, EPA and DHA, that are associated with various health benefits. EPA is helpful for reducing inflammatory responses in the body and DHA is needed, especially in puppies, for optimal neurological and visual development.

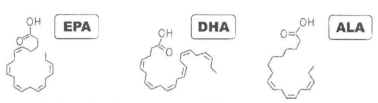

Molecular Structures of EPA, DHA and ALA

Conversely, ALA, while possibly having some independent benefits of its own, (these are not well documented in dogs), is most frequently discussed in the context of being the precursor fatty acid of EPA and DHA. The supposition is that if a food is enriched with ALA, the parent omega-3 fatty acid found in various plant sources, that it will be capable of supplying EPA and DHA because EPA and DHA will be produced in the body from the dietary ALA. Ingredient sources of ALA in a dog food include various forms of flax (more about this later), canola oil and to a lesser degree soybean oil.

Do Dogs Produce EPA and DHA? Most mammals, including dogs, can convert *some* ALA to EPA and DHA. However, adult mammals, including dogs, do not do this very efficiently. Neonates (newborn pups) are the best converters, but this ability gradually declines as puppies reach adulthood. Current evidence suggests that the ability of adult dogs to convert ALA to EPA and DHA may be too low to effectively increase EPA and DHA in the body's blood and tissues to levels that provide therapeutic benefit. For this reason, the source of the omega-3 fatty acids in a dogs' diet may be an important consideration.

Sources of EPA and DHA: Marine algae are the most efficient and the most prolific converters of ALA to EPA and DHA. Subsequently, certain species of cold-water fish (those that eat algae directly or those that consume marine creatures that eat the algae.... you know... food chains and all....), become concentrated sources of EPA and DHA. For dogs, fish oils such as salmon, menhaden and herring oil are all direct sources of the long-chain omega-3 fatty acids (i.e., they bypass need for the body to convert ALA to EPA and DHA). This fact is the reason that many dog owners regularly supplement their dog's food with some type of fish oil, most commonly salmon oil.

Levels in Your Dog's Food: A current challenge regarding omega-3 fatty acids is that optimal levels to include in dog foods are not well-defined. Additionally, both the amounts and the sources found in commercial foods vary enormously. For example, a group of researchers at the Norwegian School of Veterinary Science in Oslo, Norway measured the omega-6 and omega-3 content of 12 different brands of commercially available dog foods (1). While some foods were almost completely devoid of marine oils and the specific omega-3 fatty acids that they provide (EPA and DHA), others contained omega-3 fatty acids primarily in the form of alpha-linolenic acid supplied by plant oils. This is an important finding because only omega-3 content is reported on many pet food labels. If the omega-3 fatty acids are supplied primarily as alpha-linolenic acid, for example from flax, the health benefits that come from EPA and DHA will not be provided by that food.

Conversely, per Association of American Feed Control Officials (AAFCO) guidelines, if a pet food makes a label claim for the inclusion of EPA and/or DHA, minimum levels of these fatty acids must be reported on the food's guaranteed analysis panel. AAFCO guidelines provide a minimum level for growth foods, but not adult maintenance foods. These are 0.05% of DHA + EPA combined, which is equivalent to 10 mg/100 kcal of food.

What Should You Do? If you wish to increase your dog's intake of the long-chain omega-3 fatty acids (EPA and DHA), seek foods that report DHA and EPA levels in their guaranteed analysis panels as opposed to reporting total omega-3 fatty acids only. If you do not see these values but still are interested in feeding the food, contact the food's manufacturer. Ask how (and if) they measure DHA and EPA and ask to see those values. A minimum concentration of 0.05 % or greater is recommended. Purchase foods from manufacturers that answer your questions and readily provide you with requested information, that you trust, and that produce honest products with verified label claims.

Cited Study:

1. Alhstrom O, Krogdahl A, Vhile SG, Skrede A. Fatty acid composition in commercial dog foods. *Journal of Nutrition* 2004; 134:2145S-2147S.

9. Does supplementing with tryptophan calm anxious dogs?

Tryptophan, an essential amino acid, has long been believed to have a calming or even sedating effect upon those who consume it, either in meals or as a supplement. This belief has a storied history starting in the 1970's with a nutritionist's observation that people tend to become sleepy following indulgence in a holiday feast that includes turkey meat. It was believed that turkey meat protein contains an unusually high level of tryptophan, which is used by the body to produce serotonin (a neurotransmitter) and melatonin (a hormone). The neurological pathway through which serotonin works has anti-anxiety and calming effects and melatonin helps to induce feelings of drowsiness. Therefore, the theory goes, after consuming a meal that is replete in tryptophan, the body's production of melatonin and serotonin increase, which in turn cause drowsiness, reduced anxiety, and a calm state of mind.

Tryptophan Takes Off: The tryptophan/turkey theory became so popular and widespread in the early 1980's that nutrient supplement companies decided to by-pass the turkey part of the equation altogether and began producing and selling tryptophan supplements (L-tryptophan). These were initially promoted as sleep aids and to reduce signs of anxiety. However, as is the nature of these things, the promoted benefits of L-tryptophan rapidly expanded to include, among other things, claims that it would enhance athletic performance, cure facial pain, prevent premenstrual syndrome, and enhance attention in children with attention deficit-hyperactivity disorder.

L-tryptophan enjoyed a robust reputation as the nutrient for "*all that ails ye'*" until 1989, when it was found to be responsible for causing a disorder called eosinophilia-myalgia in more than 5000 people. At least 37 people died and hundreds more were permanently disabled. The US Food and Drug Administration quickly banned the import and sale of L-tryptophan as a supplement. Although the problem was eventually traced to a contaminant in a supplement imported from a Japanese supply company (and not the L-tryptophan itself), the ban remained in effect until 2009. Today, L-tryptophan is once again available as a nutrient supplement, but it has never regained its earlier popularity in the human supplements world.

What About Dogs? Given its history, it is odd that L-tryptophan was largely ignored by the dog world until a research paper published in the year 2000 suggested that feeding supplemental L-tryptophan might reduce dominance-related or territorial aggression in dogs (1). The researchers also studied dogs with problem excitability and hyperactivity but found no effect of L-tryptophan on either of these behaviors. However, the paper led to a highly publicized belief that tryptophan supplementation was an effective calming aid in dogs (which it definitely did *not* show in the study) and as an aid in reducing problem aggression. Today, a range of L-tryptophan supplements are marketed for reducing anxiety and inducing calmness in dogs. Interestingly, none are pure L-tryptophan, but rather also include other agents that are purported to have a calming effect on dogs, such as chamomile flower, passionflower, valerian root, or ginger.

What Does the Science Say? Does eating turkey or taking an L-tryptophan supplement reduce anxiety and induce calmness? Can this amino acid, which is an essential nutrient for dogs, be used as an effective nutrient supplement to reduce anxiety-related problem behaviors? Luckily, there is plenty of science to answer these questions.

The Turkey Myth: First, it is a myth that consuming turkey induces drowsiness or reduces anxiety. The theory fails on several counts. Most glaringly, turkey meat does not actually contain a uniquely high level of tryptophan. The amount of tryptophan it contains is similar to that found in other meats and is only *half* of the concentration found in some plant-source proteins, such as soy protein.

Second, researchers have shown that the amount of tryptophan that is consumed after a normal high-protein meal, even one that contains a lot of tryptophan, does not come close to being high enough to cause significant changes in serotonin levels in the blood or in the synapses of neurons, where it matters the most.

Finally, to be converted into serotonin (and eventually into melatonin) tryptophan that is carried in the bloodstream following a meal must cross the blood-brain barrier and enter the brain. This barrier is quite selective and only accepts a certain number of amino acids of each type. Tryptophan is a very large molecule and competes with several other similar types of amino acids to make it across the barrier. As a result, very limited amounts of tryptophan make it into the brain for conversion following a meal that includes other nutrients.

Why So Sleepy? The real explanation for the drowsiness and euphoria that we all feel following a great turkey dinner is more likely to be caused by simply eating too much (which leads to reduced blood flow and oxygen to the brain as your body diverts resources to the mighty job at hand of digestion), imbibing in a bit of holiday (alcoholic) cheer, and possibly, eating a lot of high-carbohydrate foods such as potatoes, yams, and breads, which lead to a relatively wider fluctuation in circulating insulin levels. Whatever the cause, it is most assuredly not the tryptophan.

Tryptophan Flying Solo: The erroneous focus upon turkey did have some positive consequences in that it led to a closer look at tryptophan's potential impact upon mental states and behavior when provided as a supplement. As a serotonin precursor, tryptophan (and its metabolite 5-hydroxytryptophan or 5-HTP) has been studied as either a replacement or an adjunct therapy for serotonin reuptake inhibitors (SRRIs), medications that are commonly used to treat depression in people and are sometimes prescribed as treatment for anxiety-related behaviors in dogs. Although limited work has been conducted regarding the effects of tryptophan supplementation in dogs, several informative papers did follow the initial dog study of 2000:

Tryptophan and Anxiety: Researchers at Wageningen University in the Netherlands studied a group of 138 privately owned dogs with anxiety-related behavior problems (2). Half of the dogs were fed a standard dog food (control) and half were fed the same food, formulated to contain supplemental L-tryptophan. Neither the owners nor the researchers were privy to dogs' assigned groups. In other words, this was a double-blind, placebo-controlled study, the Gold Standard of research designs. Dogs were fed their assigned diets for 8 weeks, during which time the owners recorded behavior changes. At the end of the study, the researchers also performed a set of behavior evaluations to assess the dogs. *Results:* Although blood tryptophan levels increased significantly (by 37 %) in the dogs that were fed supplemental tryptophan, neither the owners nor the researchers observed any difference in behavior between the supplemented group of dogs and the control dogs. There were moderate changes in behavior over time in *all* of the dogs, but this change was attributed to a placebo effect. Supplementation with L-tryptophan demonstrated no anxiety-reducing effects in the dogs in this study.

Tryptophan and Abnormal-Repetitive Behaviors: This was also a double-blind and placebo-controlled study (3). A group of 29 dogs was studied. Each dog had previously been diagnosed with some type of repetitive behavior problem. These included circling, anxiety-related lick granuloma, light chasing/shadow staring, or stool eating. (Note: One might question the inclusion of stool-eating in this study, since many pet professionals consider eating feces to be a form of scavenging behavior that is normal and common in the domestic dog; see Chapter 4). Dogs were treated for 2-week periods and the frequencies of their abnormal behaviors were recorded daily.

Results: The researchers reported no effect of supplemental L-tryptophan on the frequency or intensity of abnormal-repetitive behaviors. Although the owners reported slight improvements over time, this occurred both when dogs were receiving the supplemental tryptophan *and* while they were eating the control diet (there is the placebo effect again).

Tryptophan and Greeting Behaviors: Most recently, a 2018 study involved feeding adult dogs foods formulated to contain graded levels of tryptophan (4). Dogs were fed the foods for a period of 6 months and were tested every 8 weeks for behavioral responses to meeting a familiar and an unfamiliar person. *Results:* Although expected differences in responses to familiar versus unfamiliar individuals were observed, increasing dietary tryptophan had no effect on nervous or excitable greeting behaviors in the dogs during the study period.

Take-Away for Dog Folks: First, forget the turkey. While it can be a high-quality meat to feed to dogs (especially if you are selecting a food that includes human-grade meats or are cooking fresh for your dog), as a protein source turkey contains no more tryptophan than any other dietary protein. Feeding turkey to your dog will not promote calmness. Second, keep your skeptic cap firmly in place when considering the effectiveness of supplemental L-tryptophan or a tryptophan-enriched food as a treatment for anxiety-related problems. The early study in 2000 reported a modest effect in dogs with dominance-related aggression or territorial behaviors but found no effect in treating hyperactivity. Subsequently, two placebo-controlled studies reported no effect at all and the single study that reported a small degree of behavior change could not discount the possibility of a placebo effect.

Human nature encourages us to gravitate toward easy fixes for things that ail our dogs. Hearing about a nutrient supplement or a specially formulated food that claims to reduce anxiety and calm fearful dogs is powerful stuff for dog owners who are desperate to help their dogs. These types of claims are especially appealing because anxiety problems can have a terrible impact on a dog's quality of life and are often challenging to treat using the standard (and proven) approach of behavior modification. An additional risk of an inclination to accept unverified nutritional cures is that other well-established approaches such as socialization and behavior modification may be postponed or rejected by an owner who instead opts for the supplement, wasting precious time that could actually help a dog in need. Therefore, until we see stronger scientific evidence that demonstrates a role for L-tryptophan in changing problem behavior in our dogs, enjoy the turkey, but skip the tryptophan.

Cited Studies:

1. DeNapoli JS, Dodman NH, Shuster L, et al. Effect of dietary protein content and tryptophan supplementation on dominance aggression, territorial aggression, and hyperactivity in dogs. *Journal of the American Veterinary Medical Association* 2000; 217:504-508.

2. Bosch G, Beerda B, Beynen AC, et al. Dietary tryptophan supplementation in privately owned mildly anxious dogs. *Applied Animal Behavior Science* 2009; 121:197-205.

3. Kaulfuss P, Hintze S, Wurbel H. Effect of tryptophan as a dietary supplement on dogs with abnormal-repetitive behaviors. *Journal of Veterinary Behavior* 2009; 4:97.

4. Templeman JR, Davenport GM, Cant JP, Osborne VR, Shoveller AK. The effect of graded concentrations of dietary tryptophan on canine behavior in response to the approach of a familiar or unfamiliar individual. *The Canadian Journal of Veterinary Research* 2018; 82:294-305.

10. Is there a link between grain-free foods & heart disease?

Concerns about a possible connection between commercial dog foods, in particular grain-free products, and heart disease in dogs date back to mid-2018. In July of that year, the U.S. Food and Drug Administration (FDA) released an alert regarding reports of increased incidence of a heart disease called canine dilated cardiomyopathy (DCM). This disorder is characterized by weakening of the heart muscle, which leads to a decreased ability of the heart to pump, and if untreated, to cardiac failure.

Further investigation found that many of the affected dogs had reduced levels of a nutrient called taurine in their blood. These dogs responded positively to taurine supplementation. At the time, it was speculated (without evidence) that these cases were related to the consumption of foods that negatively affected the dogs' taurine status, leading to a well-known form of DCM - *taurine-deficiency* DCM. Foods containing high levels of peas, lentils, other legume seeds, or potatoes were identified as potential risk factors. These ingredients are found commonly in foods that are formulated and promoted as grain-free products.

As these things go, there followed a lot of hype and a fair bit of hysteria. Let us avoid this and instead look at the evidence – what does science tell us about the role of diet and taurine in the development of DCM in dogs and how is it that grain-free foods were targeted as a possible dietary cause?

What is Taurine? The nutrient taurine is a unique type of amino acid, called a beta-amino sulfonic acid. Unlike other amino acids, taurine is not incorporated into proteins but rather exists primarily as a free amino acid in body tissues and in blood. Taurine has many functions, but two that are important for this discussion involve its role in normal heart function and its presence as a component of bile acids. Bile acids are compounds that are produced by the liver and are needed for fat digestion.

Molecular Structure of Taurine

Most animals obtain adequate taurine to meet their needs by producing it endogenously (in the body) from two other amino acids, methionine, and cysteine. This means that while animals require taurine *physiologically*, most animals do not have a *dietary* requirement for taurine as long as their foods contain enough methionine and cysteine.

One interesting exception to this rule is the cat. Cats (but not dogs) *always* require a source of taurine in their food. If they do not have it, one of the diseases that they can develop is heart disease - specifically, DCM. Therefore, understanding the history of DCM in cats can help in untangling what was being reported in dogs.

Taurine-deficiency DCM in Cats: Looking back, I cannot avoid a sense of déjà vu. In the early 1980s veterinarians began reporting increased incidences of DCM in pet cats. By 1987, a role for dietary taurine was suspected. In a seminal study, a veterinary researcher at the University of California at Davis reported low plasma taurine levels in 21 cats with clinical signs of DCM (1). When the affected cats were supplemented with taurine, all 21 completely recovered. This discovery led to a series of controlled studies that supported the existence of taurine-deficiency DCM in cats. What is particularly intriguing and unusual about this evidence is that all of the cats who were involved were known to have been fed diets that were formulated to contain more than sufficient levels of taurine to meet cats' needs. *What was going on?*

Taurine and Bile Acids: The answer is a bit complicated and has to do with an important role that taurine plays in the body. Taurine is linked to bile acids in the liver where it forms bile salts. These compounds are secreted into the small intestine where they function to aid in fat digestion. Animals are very efficient at conserving the body's taurine by reabsorbing these bile salts back into the body further down the intestinal tract. This occurs through a process called *"enterohepatic reutilization"* and prevents daily fecal losses of taurine.

Herein lies the problem for cats (and possibly dogs) who develop DCM: If anything happens during digestion that causes the degradation of the bile salt taurine or that inhibits its reabsorption into the body, more taurine than normal will be lost in the feces. If this happens consistently, the cat will experience an *increase* in his or her daily need for dietary taurine. Simply put – if anything causes the cat to poop out more taurine-bile acid complexes (or their degraded by-products), the cat will be in danger of taurine deficiency if a higher level is not provided in the diet.

This is exactly what was happening in the cats with taurine-deficiency DCM – *and is possibly what we are seeing today in dogs*. The difference is that we know what diet factors caused taurine deficiency in cats during the late 1980s. These factors are not yet fully understood for dogs (but we can make a few educated guesses).

Here is What We Know: The studies with cats found that dietary factors could negatively influence taurine status in three different ways (2,3,4):

1. **Bile acid binding**: Certain types of dietary fiber and peptides (small protein chains) in a pet food can bind with bile salts in the small intestine and make taurine unavailable for reabsorption into the body. This results in an increased daily loss of taurine in the feces and a subsequent increase in daily taurine requirement to replace that loss.

2. **Increased microbial degradation:** Thermal (heat) processing of protein during extrusion or canning can lead to the production of Maillard end products. These are complexes of sugars and amino acids that are poorly digested in the small intestine. The undigested complexes travel to the large intestine and provide an intestinal environment that favors increased numbers of taurine-degrading bacteria. An increase in these bacterial populations reduces the proportion of taurine that is available for reabsorption and reuse by the body.

3. **Reduced taurine availability:** Third, taurine is found naturally in animal-based proteins but is not found in plant-based protein sources. Therefore, providing diets that include sufficient levels of high-quality animal proteins (that are not heat damaged) should ensure adequate taurine intake. However, protein that is of low quality or that has been excessively heat-treated will be poorly digested, reducing the availability of taurine and of its precursor amino acids, cysteine, and methionine. (**Note**: Cats produce small amounts of taurine from these precursors, while dogs can produce all of their needs from them, if adequate levels are available).

What about Dogs? One way that dogs differ from cats is that several breeds of dogs exhibit a high prevalence of taurine-deficiency DCM. Genetically predisposed breeds include the American Cocker Spaniel, Golden Retriever, Labrador Retriever, Saint Bernard, Newfoundland and English Setter (5,6,7). Individuals who are affected experience either a naturally occurring higher requirement for taurine or a metabolic abnormality that affects taurine synthesis or utilization. Additionally, large and giant breed dogs appear to be at higher risk for DCM than other dogs.

What Dietary Factors Affect Taurine Status in Dogs? Generally speaking, the dietary factors that lead to taurine depletion in cats are expected to similarly influence taurine status in dogs. The difference, however, is that unlike cats, most dogs are capable of synthesizing adequate taurine for their needs. Regardless, dietary factors that might influence a dog's taurine status include low dietary protein, poorly processed or heat-damaged protein, and the inclusion of a high proportion of plant-based protein sources and their associated fibers (see diagram on following page).

Plant-based proteins and fibers have attracted the most attention because several new types of plant-source ingredients have been increasingly used in grain-free pet foods. These ingredients include legumes such as peas, chickpeas and lentils, and tubers such as potatoes. Some commercial products contain relatively high levels of these new ingredients. The protein in these ingredients is known to be of moderate quality and is limiting in methionine and cysteine, the two precursors of taurine synthesis. Additionally, pea and potatoes contain high concentrations of a class of fermentable fibers called oligosaccharides., When included in foods, these fibers contribute to increased intestinal fermentation by gut bacteria. It has been theorized that the influences of these new plant-source proteins may cause increased degradation of taurine and/or higher losses of bile acids in the feces, thus eventually leading to a change in a dog's taurine status and possibly to an increased susceptibility to DCM.

A Few Things
ABOUT Taurine

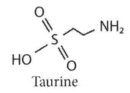

Taurine

Needed For
- Healthy Heart Function
- Component of Bile Acids
- Retinal Function
- Reproductive Health

Dietary Risk Factors for Reduced Taurine Status
- Low Protein Diet (limited taurine precursors)
- Heat Damaged or Low Quality Protein Sources
- High Dietary Fiber (e.g. rice bran, beet pulp, cellulose)
- Lamb and Rice Diets (speculated)
- Plant-based Protein Sources (peas, lentils, legumes) (speculated)

Possible Risk Factors for Taurine Deficiency DCM

Breed	Size	Diet
• St. Bernard • Newfoundland • Golden Retriever • Labrador Retriever • Amer. Cocker Spaniel	• Large breed dogs • Dogs with slower metabolic rates	• Factors that reduce taurine production • Factors that increase taurine degrading microbes • Factors that cause reduced bile acid reabsorption

In response, several research studies have examined these plant ingredients (8,9) or have compared grain-containing and grain-free foods (10). The current evidence has found that feeding peas and other legumes does not lead to decreased plasma or whole blood taurine or methionine levels in healthy dogs. Similarly, taurine status remained normal and was not affected by the presence or absence of grains in a food.

Conversely there is some evidence that the fibers that are associated with these plant-based ingredients promote increased microbial fermentation in the large intestine. A shift of this type could result in a change in the fecal bile acid profile and taurine excretion patterns. However, the impact of this change on taurine status in dogs over time is not known and needs further study. To date there is no evidence showing a connection between these ingredients and DCM in dogs. Current data suggest that these ingredients (and grain-free foods) may not be a causative factor in DCM.

Take Away for Dog Folks: Given what we currently know, a reasonable recommendation is to feed foods that contain sufficient levels of high quality, animal-source proteins. Foods that contain *only* plant-source proteins or high levels of dietary fiber should be avoided. While it is important to emphasize that there is no evidence that feeding a grain-free diet results in changes to taurine status in dogs, the potential for long-term fermentative changes in the gut to influence taurine status is noteworthy. It is possible that a shift of this type might be one of *several* different risk factors that must be in place for the development of taurine deficiency and DCM in an individual. Other factors that may be important and which require additional study include genetic predispositions, large/giant adult size, presence of overweight conditions, and age. It is quite possible (if not probable) that several different risk factors must be in place for an individual dog to develop compromised taurine status and subsequently, DCM.

Cited Studies:

1. Pion PD, Kittleson MD, Rogers QR, et al. Myocardial failure in cats associated with low plasma taurine: A reversible cardiomyopathy. *Science* 1987; 237:764-768.

2. Earl KE, Smith PM. The effect of dietary taurine content on the plasma taurine concentration of the cat. *British Journal of Nutrition* 1991; 66:227-235.

3. Hickman MA, Morris JG, Rogers QR. Effect of processing on the fate of dietary taurine in cats. *Journal of Nutrition* 1990; 120:995-1000.

4. Hickman HA, Morris JG, Rogers QR. Intestinal taurine and the enterohepatic circulation of taurocholic acid in the cat. *Advances in Experimental Medicine and Biology* 1992; 315:45-54.

5. Freeman LM, Rush JE, Brown DJ, et al. Relationship between circulating and dietary taurine concentrations in dogs with dilated cardiomyopathy. *Veterinary Therapeutics* 2001; 370-378.

6. Backus RC, Ko KS, Fascetti AJ. Low plasma taurine concentration in Newfoundland dogs is associated with low plasma methionine and cysteine concentrations and low taurine synthesis. *Journal of Nutrition* 2006; 136:2525-2533.

7. Ko KS, Backus RC, Berg JR, et al. Differences in taurine synthesis rate among dogs relate to differences in their maintenance energy requirement. *Journal of Nutrition* 2007; 137: 1171-1175.

8. Donadelli RA, Aldrich CG, Jones CK, Beyer RS. The amino acid composition and protein quality of various egg, poultry meal by-products, and vegetable proteins used in the production of dog and cat diets. *Poultry Science* 2018; October; pp. 1- 8.

9. Pezzali JG, Acuff HL, Henry W, Alexander C, Swanson KS, Aldrich CG. Effects of different carbohydrate sources on taurine status in healthy Beagle dogs. Journal of Animal Science 2020; 1-9, doi:101093/jas/skaa010.

10. Gizzarelli M, Calabrò S, Vastolo A, et al. Clinical Findings in Healthy Dogs Fed with Diets Characterized by Different Carbohydrates Sources. *Frontiers in Veterinary Science,* 8: 667 318. doi: 10.3389/fvets.2021.667318.

11. Are copper levels too high in some dog foods?

The mineral copper is an essential dietary nutrient. It is needed for the formation and activity of red blood cells, acts as a cofactor in numerous enzymatic reactions, and is necessary for normal skin and hair pigmentation. Although rare in dogs, a deficiency of copper can lead to impaired skeletal growth and anemia.

Conversely, copper *toxicity* – ingesting too much copper – may be of greater concern. Copper is stored primarily in the liver. As a result, excess copper accumulation in the body manifests as a form of liver disease called copper-associated hepatopathy. In dogs, this can be treatable if caught early. However, copper toxicosis is a serious disorder and if left untreated, can be fatal.

Genetics Matter: Copper toxicosis may have several underlying causes. The primary influencing factors include genetics, metabolic/homeostatic anomalies, and diet. For example, the Bedlington Terrier has an inherited disorder of copper metabolism that results in an inability to normally use and excrete copper. Copper toxicosis in Bedlingtons was one of the first genetic disorders to be studied by the Canine Genome Project and for which a diagnostic genetic marker was found. In this case, a simple autosomal recessive gene is responsible for the disorder.

Bedlington Terrier

Other breeds that may have genetically influenced disorders of copper metabolism include the Doberman Pinscher, West Highland White Terrier, American Cocker Spaniel, and Labrador Retriever. Less is understood about underlying genetic causes in these breeds, however.

Role of Diet: In recent years, the role of diet in the incidence of copper-associated liver disease in dogs has received attention. In early 2021, a group of six veterinarians from five veterinary teaching colleges collaborated to produce a scientific paper that tracked changes in liver copper levels in dogs and levels found in commercial pet foods (1). Here is a summary of their findings:

☙ *Changes in hepatic copper concentrations:* There are limited data regarding average liver concentrations of copper in pet dogs. However, the studies that are available span a period of almost 100 years and tell a disturbing story:

   ✓ *1929:* The first study, published in 1929, reported average hepatic liver levels of less than *10 micrograms per gram of liver (dry weight)* in dogs.

- ✓ **50 years later:** In 1982, following the introduction and widespread use of commercial pet foods, a second study reported average liver copper values of over *200 micrograms per gram* , a more than *20-fold increase.*

- ✓ **1995:** Between 1982 and 1995, the average concentration increased again; this time doubling to *453 micrograms per gram.*

- ✓ **Free-ranging dogs:** Most recently, the role of diet in liver copper concentrations was examined in a study that compared liver copper levels in free-ranging dogs in Malaysia with those of healthy laboratory dogs. The free-ranging dogs survived by scavenging human food scraps while the laboratory dogs were fed a commercial dog food that contained 23.4 mg/kg copper (a value that is within AAFCO recommendations). The laboratory-raised dogs had significantly higher liver copper concentrations compared to the free-ranging dogs. On average dogs fed a commercial pet food had more than 3-fold greater concentrations of copper in their livers, with a range of 199 to 997 micrograms per gram. For some perspective to health, dogs may develop signs of hepatic injury with liver levels as low as 600 micrograms per gram. Current recommendations to veterinarians are to treat for copper-associated liver disease when levels reach this concentration or greater.

Increased Incidence of Copper-Associated Liver Disease: The authors note that collectively, veterinary colleges have observed an increased incidence of copper-associated liver disease in dogs over the last 15 to 20 years. For example, one author examined over 2000 liver samples taken from dogs between the years 2010 and 2015. More than 50 percent of the dogs had liver copper concentrations that were classified as high – greater than 400 micrograms per gram. Additionally, many of the samples showed signs of inflammatory liver disease. Another author found that 60 percent of liver biopsies conducted at her center had high copper levels, almost all of which also showed signs of inflammatory liver disease. By any standard, these numbers are concerning.

A Dire Warning: There is no easy way to state this. The authors of this paper, six veterinary experts from independent academic institutions, believe that the changes in average liver copper concentrations and in the increased incidence of copper-associated liver disease that they are seeing are unlikely to be due to genetic factors or to changes in dogs' ability to handle/excrete copper. Rather, they theorized that diet, and specifically, commercial dog food, is the most important underlying factor influencing liver copper accumulation in dogs in recent years.

Sources of Copper in Pet Foods: Where is this copper coming from? Most pet food companies use a vitamin/mineral premix in their food formulations to properly balance products to meet AAFCO Nutrient Profiles. Prior to the late 1990's most premixes included copper in the form of *copper oxide*. However, evidence that copper oxide had a very low bioavailability in dogs (i.e., they could not absorb and use it) led to a 1997 AAFCO recommendation that copper oxide should be replaced with *copper sulfate*, a compound with higher bioavailability.

Certain pet food ingredients are also enriched sources of copper. These include organ meats (in particular liver), fish, some legumes, and even sweet potatoes. The authors speculate that the increased popularity of high protein (meat) foods and perhaps also the use of alternate carbohydrate sources such as sweet potatoes, may be another contributor to elevated copper levels in pet foods.

To Summarize: Three changes in pet food formulations over the last several decades may be influencing dietary copper levels. These are (listed in decreasing order of expected impact):

CuSO₄ **Beef Liver** **Sweet Potato**

1. Change from using copper oxide to copper sulfate in pet food vitamin/mineral premixes (1997).
2. Increased use of organ meats in high protein dog foods (and increased popularity of these foods).
3. Increased use of non-grain vegetables that are enriched sources of copper (sweet potatoes).

What IS the Dog's Copper Requirement? An exact dietary requirement for copper, as for most trace minerals, is difficult to determine because of the body's self-regulating response to need/dietary levels, to the wide range in availability among copper sources, and because of the influence of other minerals in the diet (nutrient interactions).

Given the data that we currently have, a minimum level of copper in dog foods appears to be less of a concern than is determining what is a *safe upper limit* for copper in dog foods. It is important to note that AAFCO removed their safe upper limit for copper in 2007 and has not yet provided a new value. Prior to 2007, the maximum upper limit for copper was 250 mg/kg dry diet.

Take Away for Dog Folks: First, do not panic. While the information provided in this paper is certainly concerning and is important, the take-away is *not* that dogs are universally at risk for copper toxicity. However, if you are concerned, there are a few things that you can do:

❧ ***Check copper levels:*** Reputable dog food companies provide complete nutrient analyses of their foods. While this information is not included on the pet food label, companies can provide it on their websites. The minimum copper concentration for adult maintenance foods is currently 7.3 mg/kg (dry matter basis) or 1.8 mg per 1000 kcal. The prior upper limit was 250 mg/kg. Ask about the concentration in the food that you feed and compare the value to these lower and upper limits.

❧ ***Limit foods with high copper ingredients***: Foods that are formulated with organ meats may contain naturally higher levels of copper. If you are feeding a high meat food, check levels and if you are worried, ask the company about how they are monitoring copper levels in their products.

❧ ***Talk to your veterinarian***: If you have a breed that may be at increased risk for copper accumulation in the liver or are worried about your dog's copper intake and health, first and foremost talk to your veterinarian. Ask about options for monitoring liver health and possible diagnostic procedures.

❧ ***Stay tuned***: Hopefully, AAFCO will respond to this important and timely paper and will move to ensure both sufficient minimums and safe upper limits of copper in pet foods.

Cited Study:

1. Center SA, Richter KP, Twedt DC, Wakshlag JJ, Watson PJ, Webster CRL. Is it time to reconsider current guidelines for copper content in commercial dog foods? *Journal of the American Veterinary Medical Association* 2021; 258:357-364.

12. Are we feeding dogs too much protein?

Many owners pay close attention to the protein content of the foods that they select for their dogs. This is with good reason, of course. Dietary protein is essential as the source of essential amino acids and nitrogen, and is needed by dogs for optimal growth, maintenance of healthy tissues, a properly functioning immune system and the production and functioning of all enzymatic processes in the body.

So, what actually do we know about correct dietary protein levels for dogs? How much protein is enough and are there any health risks to feeding too much?

How Much is Enough? First, keep in mind that there is not a single "perfect" value for optimal dietary protein. Multiple factors influence an individual dog's protein requirement. The most important of these include a dog's age, state of health, and activity level. Diet-related influences include a protein source's amino acid make-up, it's digestibility value, and the degree of heat- or storage-related damage that occurs during processing (more about this in later chapters).

While there is actually no single *optimal* protein level to be discovered, we do have a good idea of dogs' *minimum* protein and essential amino acid requirements. Using this information, the Association of American Feed Control Officials (AAFCO) has established two minimum protein values – one for adult dogs (maintenance foods) and a second for puppies (growth foods). These minimums are established for foods that are relatively energy dense, containing 4000 kcal/kg and that are produced using common pet food ingredients. They represent a summation of the minimum requirement plus a safety margin to account for differences in protein quality among ingredients as well as losses that may occur during processing.

- 🐾 **Maintenance Food (Adult Dogs)**: 18 percent
- 🐾 **Growth Food (Puppies)**: 22.5 percent

Today, the protein content of many commercial dog foods is considerably higher than the AAFCO minimum values of 18 and 22.5 percent. It is not unusual for an adult maintenance food to contain 30 percent protein or more – some contain as much as 40 percent protein. Why is this? Do our dogs benefit from such high levels of dietary protein? Are there any documented risks of high protein intake? Some insight comes from looking at pet food trends over the last several decades. It began more than 40 years ago with concerns about dietary protein and kidney function.

Protein and Kidney Function*:* Prior to the mid-1980's, it was generally assumed that feeding a high protein diet to dogs increased risk for the development and progression of chronic kidney disease. This theory originated from a set of studies in laboratory rats, rather than in dogs. An even greater problem was that the rat studies used male rats that had been genetically manipulated to naturally develop kidney disease.

When this theory was finally tested in dogs, it was discovered that dogs did *not* react like genetically manipulated rats. Rather, using methodologies that were available and accepted at that time, researchers found that dietary protein was not a contributing factor in the progression of chronic kidney disease in dogs. This evidence was supported by studies from separate groups and included both experimental models and examinations of dogs with naturally occurring kidney disease. Moreover, further work reported that feeding sufficient *(not* excessively high) levels of high-quality protein to dogs with mild to moderate kidney disease was helpful rather than detrimental for disease management. (*Score 1 for the high protein movement*).

Protein and Weight loss: Recent years has witnessed a dramatic increase in the prevalence of overweight conditions in dogs. In response, an entire body of research has accumulated that addresses dietary approaches to treating canine obesity. Some of this research has found that overweight dogs lose weight more efficiently when fed a high protein/low carbohydrate diet compared with when fed a diet containing more moderate levels of both nutrients. A variety of manipulations of the "high protein helps weight loss" paradigm have now been studied and have fueled a new set of over-the-counter and veterinary-prescribed foods that contain elevated levels of dietary protein. (*Point 2 for high protein*).

Carnivorous Canines: Finally, beliefs that dogs should be fed as obligate carnivores (or as wolves; pick your myth) are pervasive. Sadly, the pet food industry has jumped onto this runaway train and now produces entire brands dedicated to the belief that protein levels in foods can never be too high (nor carbohydrate levels too low). Despite the fact that dogs' actual protein needs are much lower, it is not unusual to find extruded dry dog foods with protein levels of 38 percent or more. Raw foods may have percentages that are even higher than this. Today, there is a plethora of dog food brands that target owners who desire to feed Fluffy like the domesticated predator that they long for her to be. Not surprisingly, these foods sell very well. (*It's 3 points for the win*).

Is all of this protein really needed?
Is it good for our dogs' health?

Revisiting Risks: The erratic pendulum of dietary protein may be swinging once again. A recent study, conducted by researchers at Kansas State University, examined the effects of feeding three different levels of dietary protein to healthy dogs on *metabolomics* and the gut microbiome (1).

What is metabolomics? Metabolomics, along with its close cousin, the gut microbiome, are all the rage in nutrition research these days. Metabolomics refers to the collective and analytical study of metabolites in the body. For our purposes, these are the end products of protein metabolism that are found circulating in blood or excreted in urine or feces. There are a lot of these and analysis of their trends and patterns provides valuable information about an animal's metabolic state and health.

The gut microbiome refers to all of the microorganisms naturally found in a dog's intestinal environment (see Chapter 7 for a discussion of the gut microbiome). These organisms, primarily different species of bacteria, have numerous health effects and are also a direct source of many of the metabolites that are studied in metabolomics. (Note: This is new science that was not even a glimmer of a lightbulb when the earlier protein levels and kidney function work in dogs was conducted in the 1980's and 90's).

So, what does this new study tell us about protein levels in dog food?

The Study: Healthy adult dogs were fed a low (18 %), medium (25 %), or high (46 %) protein extruded diet for 90 days. The source of the protein was dried chicken and soybean protein. The authors state in the paper that the protein sources in these foods were of high quality. Data provided in a supplemental table support this claim; protein digestibility values were ~ 90 percent.

Results: It was theorized that feeding a high protein food would lead to an increased proportion of undigested protein reaching the large intestine, where it would be subjected to degradation by gut microbes. This could subsequently impact both the gut microbiome and the dogs' metabolomics. Here are the major findings:

🐾 *Kidney function*: Metabolites that are identified as uremic toxins and associated with kidney dysfunction increased significantly in blood, urine, and feces when dogs were fed the high protein food. While some of these compounds originate from the normal breakdown of protein in the body (i.e. urea), others were *postbiotics*, compounds produced by protein-degrading bacteria in the large intestine which are subsequently absorbed into the dog's body.

🐾 *Inflammation:* Feeding a high protein food resulted in significantly higher serum and urine levels of gut-derived compounds produced by proteolytic bacteria. Two of these, indole sulfate and p-cresol are classified as pro-inflammatory compounds. Simultaneously, compounds that have anti-inflammatory properties *decreased* in serum and urine in response to feeding the high protein diet.

🐾 *Proteolytic gut microbes*: Fecal pH increased when dogs were fed the high protein food. This increase was expected and has been demonstrated in other studies. A protein-induced increase in intestinal pH indicates higher activity of proteolytic bacterial species (bugs that ferment protein) and reduced activity of saccharolytic bacterial species (bugs that ferment fiber and resistant starches). Several of the end products produced by protein-fermenting bacteria are considered to be potentially harmful. Similarly, there was a reduction in bacterial end products that are classified as beneficial when the high protein food was fed.

Take Away for Dog Folks: The authors conclude: "*These results indicate that consumption of high protein food over the long-term [results in] increases in metabolites associated with kidney dysfunction, inflammation, and proteolysis*".

It is important to emphasize (as the authors of this paper do) that while the metabolic changes that occurred when a high protein diet was fed are considered to be potentially harmful, all of the dogs in the study remained healthy. The measured indicators – metabolomic and gut microbiome changes – are still relatively new approaches to studying and monitoring dogs' response to dietary changes. Although early research concluded that protein was not a significant risk factor in the progression of kidney disease in dogs, this new research forces us to take another look at a possible connection between dietary protein and kidney function.

It is also of note that although the protein sources are not well described in this study (all that we are told is that the protein comes from some combination of dried chicken and soy protein), the digestibility data suggest that the foods contained high quality protein sources. Not to put too fine a point on this, but the negative effects of feeding a high protein diet will be exacerbated in foods that include protein of lower quality. This is expected because a higher proportion of poor-quality protein would end up in the large intestine as substrate for protein-fermenting species of bacteria.

What to Do? This evidence suggests that our dogs should be fed high quality foods that contain moderate (higher than the minimum) but not excessively high dietary protein. It should also disabuse owners of a belief that dogs need and benefit from dietary protein levels that far exceed their requirement. At a minimum, these data suggest that indeed, we can actually feed too much protein to dogs.

Up on my Soapbox

That said, time to pull out the box. Let's address the elephant in the room... Is it time to start examining issues of *over* nutrition in dogs? Here is what I mean. The study reviewed in this chapter concerned dietary protein. It asked the question – Are there health risks associated with feeding too much protein to dogs? The data suggest that there could be potential harm; specifically increases in gut microbiome-derived kidney toxins and inflammatory agents.

But, as we have seen earlier in this section, protein is not the only nutrient that we should be concerned about. In my opinion (this is a soapbox, remember), over-nutrition, providing too *much* of one or more essential nutrients, may be more of a problem today than health problems associated with nutrient deficiencies. Questions of excessive intake have been raised about several other nutrients or dietary contaminants. These include copper (see Chapter 11), mercury (see Chapter 24) and even omega-3 fatty acids. And certainly, no one can claim that the over-consumption of one of the most important nutrients, calories, is not a serious health problem in dogs today (see Chapter 6).

The pet food industry has long been held to (and has promoted) an artificial and self-created standard of "complete and balanced nutrition". This standard requires that a dog's requirement for all essential nutrients must be met by a single dog food. This expectation is rarely set for human diets. Rather, we are instructed by doctors and nutritionists to consume a variety of nutritious foods on a daily basis. For dogs, it follows that an unanticipated consequence of setting up the expectation of "complete and balanced nutrition" for foods is that products are more likely to contain an excess of certain essential nutrients than levels that are too low. Today, nutrient excesses in commercially produced dog foods may be arising as more of a health problem than are instances of nutrient deficiencies. This is an issue that is of increasing concern and in my view, requires attention and further study.

Cited Study: Ephraim E, Cochrane C-Y, Jewell, DE. Varying protein levels influence metabolomics and the gut microbiome in healthy adult dogs. *Toxins* 12(8): 517-532.

NUTRIENTS - The Science Dog Recommends

Here are several feeding tips that are suggested by new research about essential nutrients such as the omega-3 fatty acids, taurine, copper, and protein.

- ☙ Both omega-6 fatty acids and omega-3 fatty acids are needed in dogs' diets. However, the over-abundance of omega-6 fatty acids in our food supply has led to a need to pay attention to omega-3 fatty acid levels. Important omega-3 fatty acids are alpha-linolenic acid (ALA) and its long-chain derivatives, eicosapentaenoic acid (EPA) and docosapentaenoic acid (DHA). Flax is a commonly used source of ALA, while algae, fish meals and fish oils supply EPA and DHA.

- ☙ If you wish to know the level of EPA and DHA in your dog's food, check the label. Foods containing these specific fatty acids will report levels on the guaranteed analysis panel. The minimum to expect in a dry food is 0.05 % of EPA + DHA combined. Additionally, look for foods that report an omega-6 to omega-3 fatty acid ratio of 10:1 or less.

- ☙ There is evidence that average liver copper levels in dogs have increased in recent years and that rising levels in commercial dog foods may be one cause. If you are concerned about copper levels in your dog's food, check the complete nutrient profile of the food – levels should be at least 8 mg/kg (dry food) and should never approach 250 mg/kg. Ingredients that contain high levels of copper are organ meats and sweet potatoes. When in doubt, consult the company for exact values or talk to your veterinarian about your dog's liver health.

🐾 The protein content of some commercial dog foods has increased in recent years. Many foods contain substantially higher protein than dogs require. New evidence suggests that there may be several metabolic and inflammatory health risks associated with feeding too much protein to dogs.

🐾 For adult dogs, select a food that includes high quality protein sources and between 22 and 28 percent protein (dry matter basis). Avoid feeding foods that contain poor quality protein sources and an excessively high proportion of dietary protein.

Part 3 – Ingredients

13. What are protein meals and by-product meals?

Just as with human foods, processed dog foods are comprised of a set of ingredients. These ingredients are listed, in decreasing order of prevalence by weight, on the food's label. Every ingredient that is included provides a unique set of nutrients to the finished food. The majority of dry (extruded) dog foods use protein meals as the primary protein ingredient. Although label illustrations often suggest otherwise, protein meals are dried, ground products that look similar to corn meal.

Chicken Meal Used in Pet Food

Types of Protein Meal: You may see several different types of protein meals on a dog food label:

🐾 *Plant vs. animal protein sources:* Examples of commonly used plant-based protein meals are corn gluten meal, soybean meal and pea protein (see Chapter 16 for more about pea protein). In general, plant-based protein sources are an inexpensive source of protein and predominate in foods marketed to pet owners interested in economy. The quality of these meals is moderate to low in terms of amino acid balance and digestibility. Pet food companies correct amino acid imbalances in plant-based meals by combining several protein sources to ensure that all essential amino acid needs are met. Animal-source protein meals, on the other hand, vary tremendously in both source—animal species—and in quality measures such as digestibility, amino acid content and processing-related damage.

🐾 *Species vs generic group*: Animal-source protein meals may be provided as a species-specific meal or as a generic meal. Examples of species-specific meals are chicken, beef, salmon, turkey, and lamb meals. Alternatively, these ingredients may be classified more generically as poultry (contains varying amounts of chicken, turkey, or duck), fish (contains multiple fish species), or meat (contains varying amounts of pork, beef or sheep). When you see a named species as the major protein meal ingredient, it generally indicates that the food is of higher quality because ingredient supply companies are required to keep named species ingredient streams separate and designated. This translates to a more uniform product and greater regulatory oversight. Conversely, the generic term used to describe a group of food animals means that the meal may contain a mixture of species with no guarantee of any particular animal species or proportions in a given product. At the production level, this means that several ingredient streams are combined, with varying sources of origin, regulatory oversight, and quality attributes.

🐾 *Meals vs. by-product meals*: The term by-product has received a great deal of attention. Whether this is warranted or not is debatable because the distinction is largely bureaucratic. Per AAFCO guidelines, a category of by-product is only defined for chicken and poultry meals and not for any other animal protein meal. We will examine actual differences between chicken/poultry meal and their respective by-product meals shortly.

What is Rendering? The process of rendering is an intensive cooking method that converts slaughterhouse end products into a form that is acceptable for use in pet foods. Most of the animal parts used for rendering are those not typically consumed in a Western diet. These include:

- ✓ Organ meats and viscera: Spleen, kidney, liver, heart, stomach, and intestines
- ✓ Varying amounts of bone; and, in the case of poultry, necks, feet and heads
- ✓ Culled layer hens from the egg industry
- ✓ Food animals found to be too diseased or injured to pass inspection for use as human foods

Classified during the slaughter process as "inedible," these parts are redirected into an alternate supply stream and are handled, transported and processed differently than meats that are intended for human consumption.

The Process: During rendering, these various components are ground, mixed and heated to a high temperature (220° to 270° F). This cooks and sterilizes the mixture, effectively killing all microbes that are present. Sterilization is necessary because refrigeration is not required for either handling or transport of inedible foods. The resulting slurry is centrifuged at high-speed to remove fats, which are further processed and sold separately as chicken, poultry, or animal fats to be used as pet food ingredients. The mixture that remains is dried and ground to a uniform particle size that has the appearance of corn meal. Meals are low in moisture and contain between 55 and 65 percent protein, making them a rich source of protein when included in a pet food. However, the actual *quality* of that protein and the degree to which it has been heat-damaged during rendering, can vary significantly.

Why use Protein Meals? From a commercial perspective, meals are well suited for use in dry pet foods because they can be stored and transported easily and have the low moisture content necessary for extrusion processing. In extruded dry dog foods, protein meals are typically found within the first three to five ingredients on the list and provide most of the product's protein. In contrast, if a food's ingredient list shows a high-moisture protein ingredient such as chicken listed first, that ingredient only contributes a small amount of protein to the end product. Fresh meats are found first on product ingredient lists simply because ingredients are required to be listed in predominance by weight at the time of processing. Chicken contains more than 65 percent water, most of which is cooked off during the extrusion process.

Are By-Product Meals of Lower Quality? By-product meals are composed of exactly the same chicken components found in meals, with the difference that by-product meals may *also* contain varying quantities of heads, feet and viscera (guts). These body parts are prohibited by AAFCO from being included in a product that is labeled chicken meal. On the face of it, this appears to be an obvious quality distinction. After all, any product that has heads, feet and guts in it not only sounds yucky, but certainly must also be of poor quality, right?

Well … It depends.

The general (and understandable) perception of dog owners is that meals are of higher quality than by-product meals. This is clearly the conclusion that some pet food companies are counting on when they make a *"No By-products!"* claim on their label. However, actual comparisons of these two pet food ingredients have not found consistent or substantial quality differences. In reality, the inclusion of additional body parts (heads, feet and guts) in by-product meals can reduce, maintain or improve the quality of a meal (1,2).

Beaks, Feet and Guts, Oh My! These three additional parts, although certainly not very appetizing to most people, have varying nutritional value as pet food ingredients. First, the protein quality of viscera (internal organs and intestinal contents) is similar to that of chicken flesh components included in high-quality chicken meals. In other words, including organ meats and intestinal contents in a by-product meal does not negatively affect the meal's protein quality and may even improve it in poor or average quality meals. Second, the inclusion of chicken heads in the mix results in a slight reduction in nutritional quality. This is because chicken brains are highly digestible while chicken skulls, being comprised of bone, are less so. So, it appears to be a zero-sum game when it comes to the added chicken heads. Last – chicken feet. As a food ingredient that is intended to provide dietary protein, feet are simply bad and have measured quality values similar to feeding connective tissue or bone residue.

Collectively speaking, including additional body parts in a by-product meal may affect the resultant product's protein quality either positively or negatively when compared with its corresponding meal. The influence depends largely upon the actual proportion of the three different body parts that are included in the end product: If there are lots of *guts*, quality improves. *heads*: could go either way. *feet*: bad news.

So, Why All the Hype? Studies of the digestibility and protein quality of meals and by-product meals have found that as a group, meals are *slightly* more digestible and contain *slightly* more available essential amino acids than their associated by-product meals (3,4). However, there is also a lot of overlap between the two ingredient groups, meaning that a given meal may be better, equal to or even lower in quality than a given by-product meal.

Overall, the differences that have been found are neither dramatic nor worthy of the hysteria that has accompany the word "by-product" among dog owners and some pet food companies. Therefore, the marketing hyperbole and excessive "patting oneself on the back" by companies that include meals but not by-product meals should be regarded with a hefty dose of skepticism.

Cited Studies

1. Aldrich G, Daristotle L. 1988. Petfood and the economic impact. *Proceedings of the California Animal Nutrition Conference*, Fresno, CA; pp. 1140–1148.

2. Cramer KR, Greenwood MW, Moritz JS, et al. Protein quality of various raw and rendered by-products commonly incorporated into companion animal diets. *Journal of Animal Science* 2007; 85: 3285–3293.

3. Locatelli ML, Howhler D. Poultry byproduct meal: Consider protein quality and variability. *Feed Management* 2003; 54: 6–10.

4. Dozier D, Dove L. Nutrient composition of feed-grade and pet-food-grade poultry by-product meal. *Journal of Applied Poultry Research* 2003; 12:526–530.

14. Do chicken, lamb, and fish-based foods differ nutritionally?

Studies that compare the digestibility of commonly used ingredients such as protein sources like chicken, lamb, and fish, provide essential information that can help dog owners to select the best foods for their dog.

What is Digestibility? An ingredient' or food's digestibility value is a direct measure of its ability to deliver essential nutrients to the dog who is eating it. This ultimately affects not only defecation quantity and quality (how much your dog poops and how the poop looks and smells), and a dog's propensity for flatulence (no explanation needed), but more importantly, a dog's long-term health and wellness. The illustration on the following page summarizes how digestibility is measured using feeding trials with dogs.

Good vs. Poor Digestibility: The final value that a digestibility trial provides is called a *digestibility coefficient*. This term refers to the proportion of an ingredient or food that the dog absorbs into the body during the process of digestion. As a rule of thumb, foods or ingredients with digestibility values of 75 % or less are of poor quality, those with values between 75 and 82 % are classified as moderate in quality, and those with digestibility values that are higher than 82 % are of high quality. If you see products with 88 % or more reported digestibility, you have a rock star.

The paradox lies in the fact that while many pet food companies routinely measure the digestibility of their products, they are not required to report this information to the people who buy their foods. As a result, you will not see this information on pet food labels. Some companies report digestibility values on their websites, but this is still quite rare. A number of companies will not even provide this information when it is directly requested by a consumer.

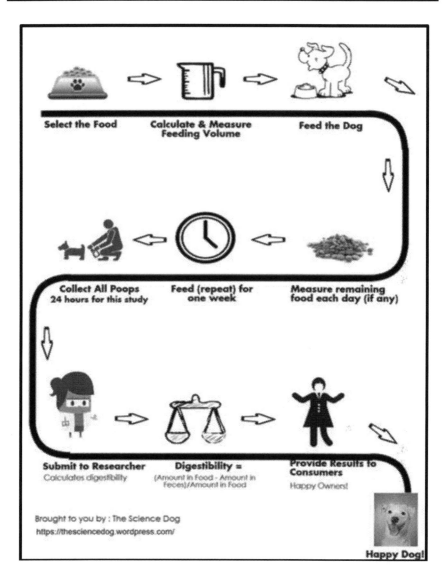

Digestibility Test Steps

The good news is that nutrition researchers at universities are also measuring these values and they *do* report what they find in the public realm (thank you nutrition researchers!). Two of these studies were conducted by nutritionists at the Norwegian University of Life Sciences and University of Copenhagen in Denmark (1,2). The first study compared the digestibility of dog foods that used three common animal protein meal ingredients (chicken, lamb, or fish). The second study compared the use of fresh chicken meat (aka "chicken first") with poultry meal as protein ingredients in a dry food.

Study 1: The investigators compared the protein and overall (dry matter) digestibility coefficients of three dry, extruded dog foods. The three foods were formulated to contain equivalent levels of either lamb meal, fish meal or poultry meal. Their results can provide some guidance for dog owners:

🐾 ***Fish meal wins:*** As a protein source in dog food, fish meal had the highest values in almost all quality measures, including digestibility and essential amino acid content. When tested in adult dogs, the protein digestibility coefficients of the three foods were *71.5, 80.2, and 87.0 percent for lamb meal, poultry meal and fish meal, respectively*. These are substantial and significant quality differences.

🐾 ***Poultry comes in second:*** Although the differences between poultry and fish meals were not as dramatic, poultry meal was found to be of lower quality than fish meal.

🐾 ***Lamb meal loses:*** The lamb meal product had the lowest digestibility value (only 71.5 %). It was also found to be deficient in the essential amino acid methionine, when digestibility was accounted for.

Overall, this study suggests that, for the sources used in this work, the order of protein quality was lamb meal (poor), poultry meal (moderate), and fish meal (high). Additionally, although the reported level of lamb meal in the diet exceeded the minimum methionine requirement for adult dogs, the actual amount of methionine that was available to the dogs (i.e., was digested) was less than the dog's minimum requirement for this nutrient.

Lamb Meal was Significantly Lower in Digestibility than Poultry and Fish Meals

---

Study 2: The team's second study examined whether or not there is a demonstrated benefit to including fresh (frozen, actually) chicken in an extruded, dry dog food. This is important because the promotion of *"fresh first"* on pet food labels is frequently used as a claim for higher protein quality. The researchers tested the digestibility and amino acid content of fresh, raw chicken (technically referred to as "raw mechanically separated chicken meat") prior to processing and then again after it was included in a dry dog food. Because raw meat has been shown to be more digestible than dry rendered protein meals, it was hypothesized that including raw chicken in the dry food would improve the food's digestibility by several percentage points. However, that is not what happened:

🐾 *Raw chicken:* As expected, when tested before processing, the digestibility of raw chicken meat was significantly greater than that of a rendered poultry meal (88.2 % vs. 80.9 %, respectively).

🐾 *Following processing:* However, surprisingly, when raw chicken meat replaced 25 percent of the poultry meal in an extruded food, the digestibility of the entire food was *not* significantly improved (81.3 % vs. 80.3 %, respectively). In addition, the digestibility of several essential amino acids was actually higher in the food containing only poultry meal than in the food that included the raw chicken meat. These results were unexpected.

🐾 *The bottom line?* When included in a dry dog food, fresh chicken meat does *not* appear to improve the food's quality in terms of its protein digestibility or amino acid availability, contrary to what numerous pet food marketing claims imply.

Take Away for Dog Folks: The results of these studies contradict several previously accepted (if never actually proven) assertions about dog food ingredients. These are:

🐾 *Lamb meal is a high-quality protein source for pet foods.* Well, apparently not. The first study found that lamb meal was poorly digested (70.5 %) and provided inadequate levels of an essential amino acid, methionine.

🐾 *Named species protein meals are always superior to generic meals.* This refers to the general rule of thumb that dog owners should always choose a food that uses chicken, turkey, salmon or lamb meals over the less specific meat, poultry or fish meals. At least regarding the animal-based protein sources used in these studies, choosing lamb over the generic poultry or fish may not get you the quality you are hoping for.

🐾 *Chicken first on the pet food ingredient label means higher quality.* Sorry, no again. While the digestibility of fresh chicken meat was better than the poultry meal prior to processing, incorporating fresh chicken into an extruded food did *not* improve digestibility or lead to a higher quality product. The researchers speculated that this may have occurred because raw meat ingredients could be more susceptible to damage caused by the heating and drying processes of extrusion than are rendered protein meals. Regardless of the cause, it appears that "Chicken First' may not be the marketing holy grail that pet food companies are promoting it to be.

Up on My Soap Box

This is helpful information for dog folks to have. Many thanks to this team of researchers, among others who have been publishing evidence about protein quality, amino acid content, digestibility and safety of various pet food ingredients and products. We are grateful and hope to see more of these types of studies.

However, I have said this many times before and will say it again. If pet food manufacturers insist on telling dog owners that their brands of food will provide *"complete and balanced nutrition"* to our dogs, then they should also be reporting a few simple measures of the quality of those foods. Apparently, the researchers of these papers agree. They finish the abstract of the first paper with this statement:

"Furthermore, the study showed that to ensure nutritional adequacy and to be able to compare protein quality of dog foods, information of [amino acid] composition and digestibility is crucial."

Indeed.

Cited Studies:

1. Tjernsbekk MT, Tauson AH, Matthiesen Cf, Ahlostrom O. Protein and amino acid bioavailability of extruded dog food with protein meals of different quality using growing mink (*Neovison vison*) as a model. *Journal of Animal Science* 2016; 94:3796-3804.

2. Tjernsbekk MT, Tauson AH, Kraugerus OF, Ahlstrom O. Raw, mechanically separated chicken meat and salmon protein hydrolysate as protein sources in extruded dog food: Effect on protein and amino acid digestibility. *Animal Physiology and Animal Nutrition* 2017; 101: e323-e331.

15. Is raw chicken more nutritious than cooked chicken?

In recent years, dog owners have become interested in selecting foods that are less highly processed. In response to these trends, nutrition researchers have started to study the effects of various types of food processing on the nutrient value of pet food ingredients. These studies provide new information regarding the effects of rendering and heat treatment on the quality and nutritional value of ingredients that we see on the pet food label.

There are two distinct attributes that are reflective of a particular protein source's quality:

🐾 *Digestibility:* High quality proteins must be digestible. Conversely, low-quality pet food proteins include those that are low in digestibility.

🐾 *Provides essential amino acids:* The protein in a dog's diet is needed as the source of essential amino acids, plus nitrogen. Essential amino acids *must* come from a dog's food. These are used by the body to produce proteins needed for growth, tissue repair, muscle development, support of the immune system and a wide range of metabolic functions. A food protein that is classified as *high-quality* is highly digestible and supplies all of the essential amino acids in proportions that are close to the dog's requirements. Conversely, protein sources that are of lower quality will be limiting (i.e., have low levels) in one or more of the essential amino acids.

Chicken Ingredients: Chicken is the most common animal-source protein used in commercial dog foods. Like many animal-source proteins, chicken muscle meat is considered to be a complete protein for dogs. This means that it can supply all of the essential amino acids in proportions that meet or exceed a dog's

103

daily requirement. The emphasis here is on the word *can*. As we will see, there is evidence that not all of the chicken ingredients found in pet foods are created equal.

Extruded pet foods use chicken primarily in the form of chicken meal, which is produced via rendering from by-products of the human food industry (see Chapter 13 for details regarding the production of animal protein meals). Chicken is also found in pet foods in the forms of frozen, retorted (canned), cooked/steamed, and raw. For most pet foods, these ingredients are all classified by the industry as pet grade (also called feed grade), meaning that they originate as by-products and are not subject to the same regulatory oversight, refrigeration, and handling requirements as are human-grade ingredients – the foods that you find in your supermarket. (We examine nutritional differences between pet-grade and human-grade foods in Section 4).

Quality Differences? The nutritional quality of chicken that is included in a pet food can be influenced by the source of the ingredients (pet grade versus human grade), product handling and transport, processing conditions, and storage. Although a number of studies have reported vast differences among dry chicken meals that are used in pet foods, there is limited work comparing raw, gently cooked, and rendered chicken ingredients. In 2019, a group of canine nutritionists at the University of Illinois provided new data by measuring the protein quality of four forms of pet-grade chicken (1). These were:

✓ Raw chicken
✓ Steamed chicken (cooked to 200 degrees F for 10 minutes)
✓ Retorted chicken (processed as in canned foods; cooked at ~ 250 degrees F for 30 minutes)
✓ Chicken meal (rendered/dried)

The Study: The researchers used a feeding assay that has been validated as a canine model for determining protein and amino acid digestibilities. Prior studies have shown that this assay's results correlate with results from feeding trials with dogs.

Results: Here are the primary findings of comparisons among raw, steamed, retorted and chicken meal:

🐾 ***Digestibility:*** The overall (dry matter) digestibility of chicken meal was significantly lower than the digestibility values of the other three forms of chicken. This difference was pronounced. Only 60 percent of the chicken meal was digestible, compared with 73 to 76 percent of the other forms. Steamed chicken had the highest digestibility value (76.5 %); this was slightly higher than that of raw chicken (75.9 %), but the difference between the two was not statistically significant.

🐾 ***Amino acids:*** Interestingly, digestibility values for all of the essential and non-essential amino acids were highest for steamed chicken – greater than 90 percent for all but two amino acids. These are rock star values if you were wondering. Raw chicken did well too – but not as well as the steamed ingredient. Across the board, the amino acid digestibility values were lowest in the rendered chicken meal. *Really low.*

🐾 ***Chicken meal inadequacies:*** The researchers found multiple essential amino acid deficiencies in the chicken meal ingredient. It was deficient in methionine, tryptophan and threonine when compared with AAFCO recommendations for adult dogs. For growth, the chicken meal met AAFCO recommendations for only three of the 10 essential amino acids.

🐾 ***Raw vs. steamed chicken:*** This study showed that moderate cooking provided a benefit over raw chicken in the form of higher essential amino acid availability in the cooked chicken. When values were compared with AAFCO recommendations for adult dogs, the steamed chicken provided significantly higher amounts of all 10 essential amino acids than did raw chicken. However, both forms of chicken met or exceeded the recommended levels and were considered to be high quality protein sources.

| Chicken Meal | Retorted Chicken | Raw Chicken | Steamed Chicken |

Take Away for Dog Folks: In this study, steamed chicken was evaluated as the highest protein quality ingredient, followed closely by raw chicken. Retorted chicken, the form that is found in canned pet foods, was of moderate quality. Chicken meal, the form of chicken that predominates in dry, extruded dog foods, lagged dramatically behind and was found to be an incomplete protein source for both adult and growing dogs. Here is a direct quote from the paper: ".... *our data indicate that if the chicken meal has a low digestibility, it may not meet the minimal recommendations for indispensable [aka essential] amino acids without supplementation, especially if the diet is formulated to meet the minimum protein requirement of the dog...*"

Up on my Soapbox

I have a bit more to say about these results.

❧ Raw vs. cooked claims: First, the pervasive belief of many who feed raw diets that raw meat (in this case chicken) provides better nutrition to dogs and that cooking meat reduces nutritional value, is not supported by these data. The moderately cooked chicken was slightly more digestible and provided higher levels of available essential amino acids than did the raw chicken. *Moderate* cooking improved nutrient availability – it did not reduce it.

❧ Chicken meal inadequacies: Conversely, the high heat treatment during rendering that is used to produce chicken meals resulted in severe reductions in protein quality. When included as the primary protein source in a food, a rendered chicken meal may not provide adequate levels of essential amino acids to growing or adult dogs. While this is probably not true of all rendered chicken meals, it was true of the source examined in this study.

❧ Food selection? The problem is that (and I have beaten this particular drum before), dog owners have very little access to information about the ingredient quality of commercial foods. Although many pet food companies measure the digestibility of their ingredients and foods, they often do not share this information. Moreover, companies are under no regulatory pressure to provide quality information about their products to consumers. As a result, in many cases, queries to companies for this information go unanswered. This is a sad state of affairs indeed.

It is time for pet food companies to provide basic digestibility information about their products to pet owners. This does not need to be complicated. Digestibility information about foods and ingredients can be easily classified into ranges. An example scale is: low (75 % or less), moderate (75 to 82 %), high (82 % to 87 %), and exceptional (88 % or more). Price points can vary accordingly of course. At the very least, pet owners should have access to meaningful information re-

107

garding the types and quality of ingredients that are included in the foods that they purchase for their dogs.

Cited Study:

1. Oba PM, Utterback PL, Parsons CM, de Godoy MRC, Swanson KS. Chemical composition, true nutrient digestibility, and true metabilizable energy of chicken-based ingredients differing by processing method using the precision-fed cecectomized rooster assay. *Journal of Animal Science* 2019; 97:998–1009.

16. Are peas and potatoes good sources of protein?

As we have seen, the source and quality of a food's protein sources are important features to consider when selecting a food. Dog owners who care about these things often agonize over how to differentiate among foods in terms of both protein level and quality. These concerns are justified because of the large number of ingredients that provide protein in dog foods and because the quality of these ingredients can vary substantially. Of interest in recent years are several novel plant-based protein ingredients that are included with increasing frequency in commercial dog foods.

Pea Protein: In 2020, a team of investigators led by Dr. Greg Aldrich at Kansas State University examine the protein quality of a large group of traditional and novel protein sources used in dog foods (1). Of particular interest was pea protein, a dog food ingredient that is relatively new to the pet food scene.

The researchers evaluated 16 different protein sources. These included various forms of egg protein (the high-quality standard by which to compare other proteins), several forms of chicken, a few common plant proteins such as soy and corn gluten meal, and two relative newbies, pea protein and potato protein. The list below describes the proteins that are of greatest interest:

✓ **Spray-dried whole egg:** In certain tests, whole egg is the standard, high-quality protein source to which other sources are compared.
✓ **Air-dried chicken:** Chicken meat dried and cooked in a hot air-drying chamber.
✓ **Low-temperature, spray-dried chicken**: By-product of the chicken fat/broth industry; cooked and dried at low temperature and pressure.

✓ **Chicken meal**: Produced by rendering of by-products from human foods industry (see Chapter 13).

✓ **Chicken by-product meal:** Same as chicken meal, but also contains varying quantities of chicken heads, feet and viscera (see Chapter 13).

✓ **Pea protein isolate**: Cooked and dried protein fraction of yellow peas.

✓ **Potato protein isolate:** Cooked and dried protein fraction of potatoes.

The researchers utilized a group of analytic measures of protein quality to evaluate each protein source. They also measured the proximate analysis of the ingredients – protein, fat, mineral (ash), moisture and fiber contents.

Results: This paper reported a lot of new information – multiple measures of 16 different protein ingredients. Here are their key findings:

🐾 *Chicken meal and chicken by-product meal*: Chicken meal and chicken by-product meal, the two most common chicken ingredients that are used in extruded pet foods, performed poorly in measures of essential amino acid content, availability, and ability to support growth. By contrast, the less heavily processed chicken ingredients, air-dried and spray-dried chicken, scored significantly higher in these measures of protein quality.

🐾 *Peas and potatoes*: The essential amino acid methionine (which is a precursor of taurine) was the limiting essential amino acid in potatoes and peas. This was not unexpected, as many plant-based protein sources are low in methionine. Overall, (again as expected), potato and pea proteins were poorer sources of the essential amino acids when compared to egg and some chicken sources. *However, in this study, EAA measures for both pea and potato protein were higher than those for the rendered chicken and chicken by-product meals* (this last bit is important).

Take Away for Dog Folks: This large study provided needed information about two commonly used dog food ingredients – chicken meal and chicken by-product meal, and also about two newcomers to the pet food scene – pea protein and potato protein.

The rendered chicken meals performed poorly in all measures of protein quality. The products that were examined in this study performed worse than egg protein (expected) and also worse in terms of amino acid measures than several plant-based proteins (not expected). Chicken meal and chicken by-product meal were also found to contain comparatively high levels of connective tissue and structural proteins, and to have low available lysine, an indicator of the types of protein damage that occur during processing. Both of these measures are indicative of a protein source that is not of high quality when fed to dogs.

Conversely, other forms of chicken, in particular the spray/air-dried forms that were cooked at lower temperatures, were found to be much higher quality protein sources. Although not commonly seen in dog foods, these are forms of chicken ingredients that should be on your watch list, as pet food producers continue to search for better quality animal-source proteins to include in their products.

Finally, pea and potato protein were both limiting in the essential amino acid methionine, which is the precursor of taurine production. Therefore, it is possible that the inclusion of these protein sources in foods, if fed without concomitantly including additional methionine or taurine or other sources of protein, may contribute to reduced taurine status in an animal. Like many plant proteins, pea and potato protein require balancing with other protein sources or amino acid supplementation to counteract their essential amino acid deficiencies.

Cited Study:

1. Donadelli RA, Aldrich CG, Jones CK, Beyer RS. The amino acid composition and protein quality of various egg, poultry meal by-products, and vegetable proteins used in the production of dog and cat diets. *Poultry Science* 2018; October; pp. 1- 8.

17. Are ancient grains a healthy alternative for dogs?

The term "ancient grains" is used to describe grain species that have not been subjected to modern breeding and selection practices. In this way, ancient grains differ from commonly used food ingredients, such as corn, wheat, and rice. Examples of ancient grains that are popular in many human foods are Kamut (the predecessor of today's wheat), millet, amaranth, quinoa, sorghum, spelt, bulgur, and oat groats.

From an environmental and sustainable standpoint, ancient grains are considered to be hardy plants that can thrive with reduced use of fertilizers, pesticides, and irrigation practices. This purportedly makes these grains more sustainable and allows production practices that result in a lower carbon footprint. When consumed as whole grains, some believe that there are health benefits associated with ancient grains.

Health of Hype? Although limited, there is some evidence for health benefits when ancient grains are included in human diets. One study found that people consuming Kamut-containing foods showed reductions in LDL cholesterol levels and had positive changes in measures of systemic inflammatory responses. Another study found that millet may dampen glycemic response and improve feelings of satiety, a change that may reduce risk of diabetes and aid in diabetic control. Some of the phytochemicals that come along with these whole grains may also have antioxidant benefits.

Regardless, beware of hype. Nutritionists and scientists are still a long way from calling ancient grains the new wonder-food (although that does not stop marketing types from making such claims). Importantly, the Whole Grains Council, a nonprofit consumer advocacy organization, suggests that the purported benefits of ancient grains have more to do with including the entire grain in foods and reduced processing than they do with any particular magical property of ancient grains. Common foods that are less highly refined, such as brown rice, whole grain pasta, oatmeal, and whole wheat bread may very well offer the same health benefits - without the exotic name and higher price tag. In other words – whole grains are good, possibly regardless of whether or not they are ancient.

What about Dogs? By now, we all know that any nutritional trend (or fad) that becomes popular in human diets will show up after a few years in dog foods. And, ancient grains have arrived, right on cue. But what do we actually know about including ancient grains in our dogs' food? Can dogs efficiently digest and utilize these grains? Are there any demonstrable health benefits to including them as ingredients in food?

Similar to their inclusion in human foods, there is not much science regarding ancient grains in dog foods. I found two studies that can help you to decide whether or not you should look for these senior starches in your dog's food.

The Five Ancients Study: The objectives of Study 1 were to examine the starch and fiber compositions and digestibility values of five different ancient grains (1). This study used a validated laboratory procedure that replicates the digestive and fermentative processes of a dog's gastrointestinal tract. Although not perfect, this approach provides valuable evidence for how well new ingredients will be digested in an actual canine stomach and intestines. In this experiment, the tested grains were amaranth, white proso millet, red millet, quinoa and oat groats.

Results: There were several differences among the five ancient grains with respect to digestibility and the type of dietary fiber that the grain provided. Regardless of these differences, all five ingredients provided a source of dietary starch that was highly digestible plus fiber that was moderately fermented, an attribute that is considered to be beneficial.

The Feeding Study: Study 2 included a group of 10 adult, female beagles who were fed dog foods that contained either amaranth, white proso millet, quinoa, oat groats, or rice (the control) as the primary starch source (2). Measurements included food and nutrient digestibility data, glycemic (blood glucose) responses, and gut microbiota changes.

Results: The ancient grains performed quite well in this study (go oldies!), with several significant findings:

- 🐾 *Digestibility values*: All five of the foods had moderate digestibility values, ranging between 82 and 86 percent. Of the four ancient grains, white proso millet had the highest digestibility value (86 %) while quinoa was lowest (82 %).

- 🐾 *Fiber*: Millet also had the highest fiber digestibility (fermentability) value, when compared to other grains. This finding suggests that millet contains a higher proportion of soluble or fermentable fibers, a difference that may be important in terms of its ability to provide prebiotic benefits.

- 🐾 *Fecal microbes*: Moderate changes were observed in several gut microbe families, but overall bacterial species richness and diversity were not impacted by feeding ancient grains.

- 🐾 *Poops:* Fecal scores (i.e., poop quality) were normal for all of the foods. Total fecal output (something that is often important to dog owners), differed though. The quinoa and amaranth-containing foods produced more feces (~68 gm/day) compared to the millet-containing food (~46 gm/day). These differences were attributed to variations in water-holding capacity, which is the ability of the starches and fibers to bind to water.

Take Away for Dog Folks: So, what does all of this mean for our dogs? Is there enough positive evidence to warrant selecting a food that contains ancient grains? Well, as with many things in life, it depends. In this case, it depends primarily on expectations.

If you are interested in selecting foods that include less highly processed (refined) grains that may be associated with a reduced environmental impact, then ancient grains could be your choice. If your goal is to provide a digestible starch source that comes along with moderately fermentable and beneficial fibers, again, ancient grains may be your starch. But remember that the more common whole grains may perform similarly in foods when fed to dogs.

On the other hand, if, as some marketing hype suggests, you expect ancient grains to be the new holy grail of food ingredients, then it would be smart to rein in those expectations. There is nothing nutritionally magical about amaranth, Kamut, oat groats, millet, or quinoa (other than perhaps being somewhat difficult to pronounce). While these grains are well-digested and accepted by dogs and provide good sources of fiber, other benefits that directly impact health and wellness have not been demonstrated in published research studies.

And not to put too fine a point on this, but most likely they never will be. Remember that ancient grains are simply early forms of domesticated grains that have not been intensively selected for hardiness, high starch content and harvesting ease. It must also be noted that no one has yet compared the nutritional performance of ancient grains with that of modern unrefined grains, such as whole grain wheat, brown rice or barley. It is quite possible that the whole grain versions of modern-day grains perform similarly to ancient grains when in the gastrointestinal tracts of dogs. Ancient grains just sound much more hip than whole wheat.......

116

Cited Studies:

1. Traughber ZT, He F, Hoke JM, Davenport GM, de Godoy MRC. Chemical composition and in vitro fermentation characteristics of ancient grains using canine fecal inoculum. *Journal of Animal Science* 2020; 98:1-8. doi:10.1093/jas/skaa326.

2. Traughber ZT, He F, Hoke JM, Davenport GM, de Godoy MRC. Ancient grains as novel dietary carbohydrate sources in canine diets. *Journal of Animal Science* 2021; 99; doi.org/10.1093/jas/skab080.

18. What is flax and should it be in my dog's food?

The three fatty acids in the omega-3 family that are important nutritionally are the parent fatty acid alpha-linolenic acid (ALA), plus its long-chain derivatives, eicosapentaenoic acid (EPA) and docosahexaenoic acid (DHA).

ALA
Alpha-Linolenic Acid

SDA
Stearidonic Acid

EPA
Eicosapentaenoic Acid

DHA
Docosahexaenoic Acid

It is these two latter fatty acids, EPA and DHA, that are associated with various health benefits. EPA is helpful for reducing inflammatory responses in the body and DHA is needed, especially in puppies, for optimal neurological and visual development.

As we learned in Chapter 8, ALA, while possibly having some independent benefits of its own, is most frequently discussed in the context of being the precursor fatty acid of EPA and DHA. However, the ability of adult dogs to convert ALA to EPA and DHA may be too low to effectively increase the long-chain and beneficial omega-3 fatty acids in the body's blood and tissues. For this reason, the source of the omega-3 fatty acids in a dogs' diet becomes an important consideration. This brings us to a common ingredient in commercial pet foods – flax.

EPA and DHA Ingredients: Marine algae are the most efficient and the most prolific converters of ALA to EPA and DHA. Subsequently, certain species of cold-water fish and the oils from those fish are concentrated sources of EPA and DHA (see Chapter 8). For dogs, fish oils such as salmon, menhaden and herring oil all are direct sources of the long-chain omega-3 fatty acids, which bypass the need for the body to convert ALA to EPA and DHA.

Flax in Pet Foods: In light of this, why then are flax and flaxseed oil so frequently promoted as a beneficial source of omega-3 fatty acids in foods or for use as a dietary supplement? Flax is a concentrated source of ALA but contains no EPA or DHA. It is included in commercial pet foods because it is an inexpensive and sustainable way to increase a product's concentration of total omega-3 fatty acids. The presumption has been that, as a source of ALA, flax effectively leads to increased EPA and DHA in a dog's blood and tissues. This presumption is a bit fishy (don't you agree?) since we know that dogs are not very efficient converters of ALA to EPA and DHA.

However, until recently, we did not have *data* showing what the difference between feeding flax and other omega-3 fatty acid sources to adult dogs might be. A study conducted in 2021 examined the effects of feeding a food that was enriched with flaxseed oil on the EPA and DHA status of healthy adult dogs (1). Here is what they did:

The Study: The researchers' objectives were to study the effects of feeding either a source of ALA (flaxseed oil) or a source EPA and DHA (krill oil) on dogs' omega-3 status. Twenty adult Alaskan Huskies were fed the same complete and balanced dog food; 10 dogs were supplemented daily with flaxseed oil to supply 1.068 mg of ALA and 10 dogs were supplemented with krill oil to supply 1.15 mg of EPA/DHA. Blood fatty acid levels and omega-3 content in red blood cells were measured at the start of the study (Week 0), midway through (Week 3) and at the end of the study (Week 6).

Results: EPA and DHA status increased significantly in dogs fed supplemental krill oil, but *not* in the dogs fed supplemental flaxseed oil. This difference was quite dramatic; the total omega-3 status (called Omega-3 Index) increased by more than 60 percent (1.68 % to 2.7 %) in the dogs fed krill oil. In contrast, the index in dogs fed flaxseed oil decreased significantly during the study period, going from 1.6 % to 0.96 %.

Take Away for Dog Folks: These results provide impressive evidence that feeding flax to dogs is not an effective means of enhancing omega-3 fatty acid status, when the goal is to increased EPA and DHA levels in tissues. If your intent is to enhance your dog's EPA and DHA status, the ingredient source on the pet food label is an important consideration. A food that includes a marine source of omega-3 fatty acids is more likely to provide the long-chain omega-3 fatty acids to your dog than are plant-based sources such as flaxseed or flax oil.

Cited Study:

1. Dominguez TE, Kaur K, Burri L. Enhanced omega-3 index after long- versus short-chain omega-3 fatty acid supplementation in dogs. *Veterinary Medicine and Science* 2021; 7:370-377.

19. Do salmon & krill differ as omega-3 fatty acid sources?

As a recap, it is probably beneficial to increase the proportion of omega-3 fatty acids in our dogs' diets. This is best accomplished by feeding foods with a reduced proportion of omega-6 fatty acids (though NOT eliminating them altogether because linoleic acid, the parent omega-6 fatty acid is an essential nutrient for dogs), and that contain an increased proportion of omega-3 fatty acids. Because foods produced with our current agricultural systems result in high levels of dietary omega-6 fatty acids, focus generally centers on increasing the omega-3 fatty acid family.

Not Flax: We also know from the previous chapter that because adult dogs are inefficient converters of ALA to EPA and DHA that flax is not a good source of the long-chain omega-3 fatty acids for dogs. Rather, certain types of fish oils (and microalgae) are identified as good sources. This brings us to yet another newcomer to the dog food ingredients market – Krill.

Why Krill? Krill are small crustaceans that are found in all the world's oceans and include more than 80 separate species. The species that is used commercially is the Antarctic krill, *Euphausia superba*, which looks like a small shrimp.

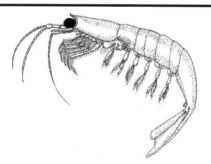

Antarctic Krill (*Euphausia superba*)

Krill feed on phytoplankton (microscopic algae) and are a primary food source for many larger animals, including baleen whales, penguins, and seals. Commercially, krill are used in the aquaculture industry and to produce fishing bait. In recent years, krill meal and krill oil have been studied as sources of protein and long-chain omega-3 fatty acids in pet foods.

Form Differences: As omega-3 fatty acid sources, there is an important difference between fish oil and krill. Fish oil fatty acids are found primarily in the form of triglycerides – three fatty acids attached to a molecule of glycerol.

Molecular Structure of a Triglyceride

Conversely, the fatty acids present in processed krill are primarily in the form of phospholipids. These structures differ in the presence of a phosphate group in one of the fatty acid positions on the glycerol molecule. For our purposes, it is important to know that phospholipids are the form of fatty acids that are incorporated into cell membranes. This means that they are already present in the structure that the body uses, when supplied as krill.

Does this Difference Matter? This is the question at hand. There is some evidence in human subjects and laboratory animals that the long-chain fatty acids that are found in krill oil, because they are in the form of phospholipids, may be more efficiently utilized by the body than those supplied by other fish oils, which come in the form of triglycerides. The practical implication of this is that the dose that is needed to increase omega-3 fatty acid levels in the body may be significantly lower when supplied as phospholipids (from krill) compared to the dose needed when supplied as triglycerides (fish oil). Recently, this hypothesis was studied in dogs (1).

The Study: Researchers designed a study to evaluate the ability of krill meal versus fish oil to increase omega-3 fatty acid status in a group of healthy adult Alaskan huskies. A group of 20 dogs was divided into two groups of 10 dogs each. All of the dogs were fed the same complete and balanced commercial dog food. Group 1 was fed a krill meal supplement providing 1.7 grams of EPA/DHA per day. Group 2 was fed a fish oil supplement providing the same amount of EPA/DHA. Dog were fed the supplements for six weeks and omega-3 fatty acid status was measured at baseline, 3 weeks, and 6 weeks.

Results: The Omega-3 Index increased in both groups of dogs. However, this increase was significantly greater in dogs fed krill oil compared to those fed fish oil (62 % vs. 21 % increase from baseline). The change in the krill meal group was driven primarily by EPA (eicosapentaenoic acid), rather than by DHA (docosahexaenoic acid). This occurred because krill provides a rich source of EPA but is lower in DHA than are most fish oil supplements. In contrast, dogs fed fish oil showed a slight but statistically significant increase in DHA levels compared to dogs fed krill meal.

Take Away for Dog Folks: So, what do these results signify in a practical sense? First, like fish oil, krill meal supplies a concentrated source of long-chain omega-3 fatty acids to dogs. These data also corroborated studies in other species demonstrating that omega-3 fatty acids were more efficiently supplied by krill oil compared to fish oil. There was a simultaneous reduction in omega-6 fatty acids in dogs fed krill meal, specifically in arachidonic acid (AA). This change *suggests* a potential shift towards reduced production of pro-inflammatory mediators. However, remember that this last step has not yet been demonstrated, nor are there any clinical trials showing reduction in inflammatory disease in dogs fed krill meal or krill oil. (In other words, take care to not over-interpret these results).

Second, should you feed krill oil (or meal) rather than fish oil? Well, the jury is still out on this one. Both krill and fish oils can effectively increase omega-3 fatty acid status in dogs. Krill just may accomplish this more efficiently. Krill is often promoted as a more sustainable source of omega-3 fatty acids (and possibly an alternative protein source) for dogs due to the use of eco-friendly harvesting. However, others argue that these methods are offset by the resource-heavy processing methods used with Krill. At this point, take these data for what they tell us. Krill is a potentially more sustainable source of omega-3 fatty acids that may be more efficiently utilized by dogs when compared to fish oils.

Cited Study:

1. Burri L, Heggen K, Storsve AB. Higher omega-3 index after dietary inclusion of omega-3 phospholipids versus omega-3 triglycerides in Alaskan Huskies. *Veterinary World* 2020; 13:1167-1173.

20. Is insect protein a nutritious and safe pet food ingredient?

Insect protein as an alternate and renewable protein source is a hot topic these days. Numerous human cultures around the world have historically viewed insects as acceptable and even desirable food items. With the ever-expanding human population and an increasing need for sustainable food sources, various forms of insect ingredients are being considered as foods for both humans and dogs.

Insect Protein: Protein is the most expensive nutrient in the diet of all animals, including humans. It is expensive both in terms of the monetary cost of its production and its ecological impact upon the environment. In the spirit of sustainability and with the goal of reduced production costs, pet nutritionists have been studying several insect species as potential alternative protein ingredients for pet foods.

Before your "ick" response leads you to stop reading, just consider a few facts regarding insect-based protein sources:

* *We eat bugs:* It is estimated that nearly one-third of humans on the planet regularly include insects in their diet. The larval forms of many species can provide a rich source of high-quality protein and fat, at levels similar to those found in meat and fish.

* *Insects are environmentally friendly*: Compared with meat sources of food protein, insect farming is highly efficient and requires less land, water, and feed resources.

* *Insect proteins appear to meet dogs' needs:* A study of multiple insect species compared the amino acid content of insect protein with the NRC amino acid requirements of dogs

125

and cats. The researchers found that almost all of the species that they examined contained sufficient concentrations of protein, essential amino acids, and taurine to meet or exceed the NRC requirements for growth for dogs and cats (1).

Regardless of the hype, there are still a relatively limited number of controlled studies that have examined the digestibility, nutrient content, and safety of feeding insect protein to dogs. Here are summaries of what we currently know:

Is Bug Protein of High Quality? In addition to the amino acid study mentioned above, another team of nutritionists compared the in vitro (in laboratory) protein quality of a range of different insects (2). They examined several of the life stages of houseflies, black soldier flies, crickets, meal worms, roaches, and cockroaches. In case you need a primer on a bug's life, here is a general review:

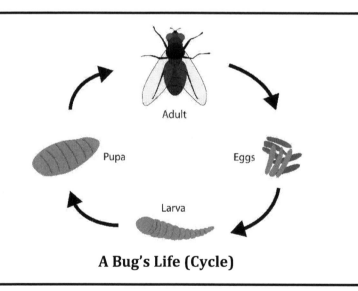

A Bug's Life (Cycle)

They compared these different bug protein sources to the meat protein sources that are commonly included in dog foods – poultry meal, fish meal and soybean meal. They found that bug crude protein levels varied between ~ 45 and 65 percent of dry matter, with adult crickets having the highest concentration. These levels were similar to those reported in fish and poultry meal and somewhat higher than levels in soybean meal. Two insect proteins that were rated as high quality were the pupae stages of houseflies and black soldier flies. *Adequate protein quality? Probably.*

Can Dogs Digest Bug Protein? When tested using a laboratory model, the protein digestibility of black soldier fly larvae and yellow meal worms were 89 and 92 percent, respectively (3). These values are comparable to those of high-quality animal protein meals. When actually fed to dogs, an extruded dry dog food containing black soldier fly larvae as its primary protein source had higher digestibility values than the control food that contain venison meal (4). The nutrient content of the two foods was similar, but the insect-containing dog food was significantly more digestible than the animal-protein containing food. Protein digestibility values were lower than the reported in vitro values, but still quite respectable. When a second group of researchers fed dogs foods containing up to 24 percent cricket meal, all levels of cricket protein supported normal gut health, feces production and gut microbiome diversity (5). Finally, using an in-home feeding study, owners of dogs who were fed a food containing meal worm protein as the primary protein source did not notice any difference in feces frequency or quality in their dogs (6). *Digestible? Yes.*

Will Dogs Eat Bug Protein? This one is a bit of a no-brainer, actually; written by someone whose dogs happily snarf up anything they can find, catch or smell whilst rooting about on walks. Regardless, this is an important question, especially for pet food producers. All of the previously noted studies reported high diet acceptability. In addition, when researchers specifically targeted dogs' olfactory (scenting) reactions to three insect species that are used in foods (crickets, black soldier flies, meal worms), the dogs were as attracted to the bug smells as they were to the control scent which was a dry, extruded dog food (7). *Tasty to dogs? Of course.*

Will Owners Accept Bug Protein? The jury is still out on this one, especially in the United States. While the companies that are testing insect-based dog foods are collecting this type of data, there are no published studies to date (nor would I expect any soon, unless an independent researcher conducts a study). *Owner acceptance? Unknown.*

Is Eating Bugs Safe? Personally, for me, this is the most concerning question of all. Although there are insect-containing foods (and many treats) already on the market, there are no long-term safety studies of any of these ingredients. The longest feeding study that has been reported lasted only 42 days – a bit longer than a month. Given the common but questionable industry practice of advising owners to feed a single brand of food to their dog throughout the dog's natural life, 42 days does not seem to be adequate for ensuring dogs' safety and long-term health. Similar to other novel pet food ingredients, it can be argued that we need additional safety studies to ensure that long-term health is supported with these new forms of dietary protein. (Clearly, this one bugs me a bit....). *Long-term safety? Unknown.*

Take Away for Dog Folks: The information that we currently have tells us that certain insect protein sources, specifically black soldier fly larvae, crickets, and yellow meal worms, can provide an acceptable and digestible protein source for dogs. The exoskeleton material, chitin, that comes along with bug protein may also provide a source of non-fermentable fiber. Given that our current animal protein production methods are not sustainable and that insects already make up a substantial part of human diets worldwide, it seems that including insect protein in dog foods may be an acceptable and sustainable solution. Still, it may be prudent to wait for a few more studies that include longer periods of feeding and the inclusion of standard measures of health before jumping completely onto the insect bandwagon. Hopefully, we will see these soon.

Cited Studies:

1. McCuster S, Buff PR, Yu Z, Fascetti AJ. Amino acid content of selected plant, algae and insect species: A search for alternative protein sources for use in pet foods. *Journal of Nutritional Science* 2014;3:e39;1-5.

2. Bosch G, Zhang S, Oonincx AB, Hendriks WH. Protein quality of insects as potential ingredients for dog and cat foods. *Journal of Nutritional Science* 2014; 3:e29;1-4.

3. Bosch G, Vervoort JJM, Hendriks WH. In vitro digestibility and fermentability of selected insects for dog foods. *Animal Feed Science and Technology* 2016; 221:174-184.

4. Russo N, Pagani E, Schiavone A, et al. In vivo and in vitro digestibility of extruded dog foods with *Hermetia illucens*. *Italian Journal of Animal Science* 2019;18;s1; 107.

5. Jarett JK, Carlson A, Serao MR, et al. Diets with and without edible cricket support a similar level of diversity in the gut microbiome of dogs. *Peer J* 2019;7:e7661, DOI 10.7717/peerj.7661.

6. Leriche I, Fournel S, Chala V. Assessment of the digestive tolerance in dogs of a new diet based on insects as the protein source. *Proceedings of the 21st European Society of Veterinary and Comparative Nutrition Congress, er* 2017;p. 203.

7. Kieronczyk B, Rawski M, Pawelczyk P, et al. Do insects smell attractive to dogs? A comparison of dog reactions to insects and commercial feed aromas – a preliminary study. *Annals of Animal Science* 2018; 18:795-800.

INGREDIENTS - *The Science Dog Recommends*

Here are a few helpful tips that we can glean from research about ingredients used in pet foods today:

☙ Protein meals provide almost all of the protein in dry (extruded) dog foods. To determine the primary protein sources in a food, look for meals or by-product meals that are listed in the first three to five items on the ingredient list.

☙ If a dry food's ingredient list shows a high-moisture ingredient such as chicken or turkey first, remember that this ingredient may contribute a small amount of protein to the end product. Fresh meats contain more than 60 percent water, most of which is cooked off during the extrusion process.

☙ Moreover, these ingredients do not necessarily translate to a higher quality product. Evidence shows that adding a bit of fresh meat to an extruded food does *not* improve digestibility or lead to a higher quality product.

☙ Quality differences between protein meals and by-product meals are not consistent. What is more important is the source, handling and processing of the dry meals that are used in dog foods.

☙ Contrary to popular belief, lamb meal is not a high-quality source of protein when included in dry dog food. A study reported very low digestibility of a lamb meal-based food and found that lamb meal provided inadequate levels of the amino acid, methionine. In contrast, fish meal and poultry meal were of higher quality when compared to lamb meal.

- Moderate cooking or steaming of chicken does not negatively affect its nutritional value. Conversely, heat processing associated with the production of dry chicken meals and extrusion can lead to severe reductions in protein quality.

- Despite popular marketing campaigns, there is nothing nutritionally superior about the ancient grains such as amaranth, Kamut, oat groats, millet, or quinoa. When included in dog foods, the starch in these grains is highly digestible. Like other whole grains, these ingredients also provide a good source of fiber. However, specific health benefits of ancient grains have not been demonstrated.

- Including flax or flaxseed oil in dog food is not an effective means of enhancing a dog's EPA and DHA fatty acid status. Rather foods that includes a marine source of omega-3 fatty acids are more likely to achieve this.

- Both krill and fish oils can effectively increase omega-3 fatty acid status in dogs, although krill may accomplish this more efficiently. Because of eco-friendly harvesting methods, krill oil may also be a more sustainable source of omega-3 fatty acids.

- If you are unsure about the quality of the ingredients of a commercial product, contact the pet food producer and request basic digestibility information. Reputable companies should provide this information. As a general rule of thumb, foods can be classified into the following groups in terms of dry matter digestibility values: Poorly digested (75 % or less), moderate (75 to 82 %), high (82 % to 87 %), and exceptional (88 % or more).

- Although long-term feeding studies are needed, current evidence shows that insect protein sources such as black soldier fly larvae, crickets, and meal worms, can provide acceptable and digestible protein sources for dogs.

Part 4 – Foods

21. What does "natural" actually mean on dog food labels?

The sale of dog foods that carry a claim of *natural,* either embedded into their brand name or on their front label, has exploded during the last decade. The sale of foods that are marketed in this way more than doubled between 2008 and 2012 and has continued to rise annually since then. Today, dog foods that *lack* the word natural on their label are actually more uncommon than those that include it.

So, what is all of the fuss about? Does a claim of "natural" mean anything for your dog or is it just one more marketing gimmick to be wary of?

Natural Claim on a Dog Food Label

The Definition: The Association of American Feed Control Officials (AAFCO) is the organization that sets pet food ingredient and labeling definitions in the United States. AAFCO standards state that a pet food manufacturer can include the word *natural* in a product's brand name or as a label claim if the food has been preserved using only non-synthetic (i.e., naturally derived) preservatives. This means that the food cannot include artificially produced compounds such as butylated hydroxyanisole (BHA), butylated hydroxytoluene (BHT), tert-butyl hydroquinone (TBHQ), or ethoxyquin. Instead, naturally derived preservatives such as tocopherols (vitamin E), ascorbic acid (vitamin C), citric acid, and rosemary extract are used. In today's pet food market, this is not a high bar to clear. Starting in the 1980's, consumer pressure to eliminate the use of ethoxyquin in pet foods was followed by a general trend away from artificial preservatives. Today almost all pet food manufacturers produce at least one product line of foods that are preserved without synthetic compounds and legally carry the "*All Natural*" claim.

In Practice: The AAFCO definition of the term natural is so incredibly broad that it includes nearly every single type of pet food ingredient that is currently included in commercial pet foods, with the exception of chemically synthesized vitamins and minerals. And even with these, there is a bureaucratic loophole. A manufacturer that includes these items can still use the natural moniker provided the statement "*with added vitamins and minerals*" is tacked onto their "All Natural" claim.

What Natural is Not: It is important to understand that a label claim of natural does *not* signify anything about a dog food's quality, the source of ingredients that it includes, the company's manufacturing practices, or the food's safety record. Neither does the appearance of the word *natural* signify that a food is organic, that it does not contain genetically modified ingredients, or is made from human-grade ingredients. The bottom line is that other than ensuring that the food does not contain synthetic preservatives, a label claim of natural is meaningless and provides little information that can help a dog owner to differentiate among foods in terms of quality, digestibility, manufacturing practices or food safety.

134

Natural vs. Organic: There *is* however an important distinction between the terms natural and organic when they are included on a food's label. According to the USDA's National Organic Standards Board (NOP), a food can be labeled organic if the plant ingredients that are included were grown without pesticides, artificial or sewage sludge fertilizers, or irradiation, and exclude genetically modified organisms (GMOs). Animal-source ingredients must come from animals that were raised exclusively on organic feed, were not treated with hormones or antibiotics, and were housed and fed according to animal welfare standards.

However, these requirements were developed for human foods, not for pet foods and AFFCO has not yet developed regulations that oversee organic pet foods. Currently, pet food companies are allowed to voluntarily choose to meet the NOP standards for human foods and can apply for NOP certification. If accepted, the company can then use the USDA Organic seal on their label.

USDA Organic Seal

If you wish to feed an organic food, these are the statements that you should look for:

🐾 *"100 Percent Organic"* means that every single ingredient must be organic.

🐾 "*Organic*" dog foods must include at least 95 percent organically produced ingredients.

🐾 "*Made with Organic Ingredients*" means that at least 70 percent of the product's ingredients are organic.

Why Natural? Oddly enough, despite the fact that the term organic is clearly defined and is better regulated than the term natural, it is the natural foods segment and not organic pet foods that have taken off in pet food sales. A marketing research study examined these differences and asked why (1).

The Study: Marketing researchers at New Mexico State University surveyed a group of 661 U.S. dog owners regarding their pet food choices. The researchers presented participants with a panel of dog foods that varied in key attributes such as price, ingredient type, label claims, and package size and asked them to identify the food that they would choose for their dog. The objectives of the study were to test the effects of label claims such as "*Veterinarian Recommended*", "*Natural*" and "*Organic*", among others. Because a primary goal was to study perceptions of natural pet foods, the participants were provided with the AAFCO definition of the term natural and with the USDA definition of the term organic prior to starting the survey.

Results: Of the dog food attributes that were studied, the price of the food was found to be the most important determinant of choice. Following product cost, owners focused most intently upon whether or not the food's ingredients were promoted as being natural or organic. When these two ingredient types were compared, dog owners were willing to pay the highest price for a dog food containing a claim of natural ingredients, more so even than for a food stating that it contained organic ingredients. Following price point, the most important driver for choosing a dog food was seeing the word natural somewhere on the food's label or in its brand name.

Take Away for Dog Folks: Perhaps the most important fact that dog owners should be aware of is that virtually anything goes when it comes to the *"It's Natural"* claim on pet food labels. (This is also true of human foods, by the way). The only significant requirement that a dog food labeled as *"All Natural"* has is that it cannot contain artificial preservatives.

Even knowing the broad definition of the term natural, people continued to attribute great value to the term and showed that they were willing to pay a premium price to see it on their dog's food label. In fact, the study showed that owners were willing to pay *more* for natural ingredients than for organic ingredients despite learning just minutes earlier about the clear differences between the two terms and the stricter guidelines for and regulation of organic foods. Have no doubt about it; this distinction is a win-win for pet food manufacturers because the cost difference between making an *"All Natural"* pet food claim that means very little and an *"Organic"* claim that is associated with set guidelines is substantial.

Expect to see even more of the word natural on pet food shelves in the future. And train yourself to ignore it. Pet food claims for providing superior nutrition, for promoting health, or for being safer do not *follow* from a claim of naturalness without actual evidence of such benefits. This is especially true when the word means nothing at all in the first place.

Cited Study:

1. Simonsen JE, Fasenko GM, Lillywhite JM. The value-added dog food market: Do dog owners prefer natural or organic dog foods? *Journal of Agricultural Science* 2014; 6:86-97.

22. Are health claims for pet foods well regulated?

Marketing researchers study promotion strategies to determine the types of advertisements that will successfully increase sales of their products. This is no less true for pet foods than it is for any other consumer goods. Some of the more obvious approaches that are used to attract dog owners to a particular brand are advertisements that appeal to our emotional attachment to dogs, capitalize on our desire for expert approval, or exploit our fascination with the lives of celebrities.

So, pick your poison – there is a dog food advertising campaign out there designed to appeal to just about every dog owner demographic. Even though each and every one of us will insist that these schemes do not work on us (and that we select a dog food based solely upon its nutrient content, ingredient quality and suitability for our dog, thank you very much), these campaigns do indeed work very well.

Marketing's Holy Grail: Advertising campaigns that have been shown to increase human and pet food sales more than any other are those that include *health claims*. The types of claims that companies can make about their products are broad, cover a myriad of chronic health problems, and have relatively loose regulatory oversight. In the United States, the wide acceptance of health claims on human food labels has occurred because of the cumulative effects of a series of three laws that were passed in the 1990's. These laws radically curtailed regulatory oversight of health claims on nutritional supplements and packaged foods, leading to labels that include a wide variety of health-related assertions for people. Examples include improved immune function, supported intestinal health, better heart health, and even prevention of cancer. If the claims employ acceptable phrasing, food companies are under absolutely no regulatory pressure to provide scientific evidence that supports the claims.

Dog Food Health Claims. Commercial dog foods are no different. As it stands today, pet food companies may include a range of general health claims on their labels with no legal obligation to substantiate the claims. *In other words, they neither have to prove the claim nor provide any evidence supporting the claim to any regulatory agency.* Marketers must simply word their brand name or advertisement carefully enough to prevent the FDA from considering it to be a drug claim (which *is* regulated). The difference between a general health claim (allowed and no proof needed) and a drug claim (not allowed; regulated by FDA) for pet foods turns on just a few words and phrases. Examples are provided in the table below:

ALLOWED	PROHIBITED (DRUG CLAIM)
❧ Supports healthy skin & shiny coat ❧ Promotes a glossy coat	❧ Reduces skin flaking & itchiness ❧ Prevents skin problems ❧ Hypoallergenic
❧ Supports healthy joints & mobility ❧ Glucosamine & chondroitin sulfate help to maintain cartilage health	❧ Reduces signs of arthritis & pain ❧ Prevents progression of joint disease ❧ Reduces joint inflammation
❧ Veterinarian recommended ❧ Veterinarian formulated ❧ Veterinarian developed	❧ Veterinary Approved - legal term is "approved" because veterinarians do not officially approve labels or products

Are These Claims Confusing to Consumers? A group of researchers at Tufts University's Cummings School of Veterinary Medicine asked exactly this question. They examined the nutrient profiles and ingredient lists of 24 brands of dog food that are promoted as beneficial to skin and coat health (1). The objective of their study was to identify consistencies and inconsistencies among commercial products that include pet health claims on their labels.

Results: They examined 15 dry (extruded) foods and 9 canned foods, representing 11 different brand names. Here is what they found:

🐾 *It's all in the name:* All 24 products included the terms skin and coat, plus a descriptor of skin/coat health in the brand name. They also included additional health-related terms on their label and website that were not restricted to skin and coat. The most commonly used phrases were *sensitive, skin sensitivities, digestive sensitivity, digestive health,* and *limited/ unique ingredients.*

🐾 *Ingredients*: If you believed these foods would contain a handful of specific ingredients that are known to be beneficial to canine skin and coat, think again. Protein sources in the 24 foods were all over the map and included chicken, fish, egg, venison, beef, pork, duck, lamb, soy, peas, and turkey. A similar cornucopia was found for carbohydrate sources, with rice, potato, wheat, oats, barley, millet, corn, quinoa, and tapioca all making an appearance.

🐾 *Not so special fatty acids:* Thirteen of the 24 foods (54 %) identified fatty acids as nutrients that are important for skin and coat health. While this may be true for certain specific omega-6 and omega-3 fatty acids (and their ratios), 10 of the 13 foods did not identify these by name. Instead, they used vague (and meaningless) terms such as "*omega fatty acids*" or "*omega oils*". Less than one-third of the foods provided

140

information about the amount of any specific fatty acid in the food. When this information was supplied, the range in EPA and DHA (as we know, the two most important omega-3 fatty acids) concentrations overlapped with those found in foods not labeled for skin/coat health.

🐾 *More nothin' special:* The essential nutrient content and caloric density (number of calories per cup) of the 24 foods varied enormously and overlapped with other brands that are sold for adult dogs but are not specifically marketed for skin health. In other words, not to put too fine a point on it, there was *nothing* that was consistently special or unique about the nutrient content of these foods. Even omega-3 fatty acid concentrations varied tremendously, making claims of *"Source of Omega-3 Fatty Acids"* essentially useless to consumers.

Conclusions: The researchers were rather circumspect in their conclusions, stating that the wide variety of ingredients and large range in nutritional value of products marketed for skin and coat health make product selection for owners who are interested in these foods confusing.

Personally, I am going further than "confusing".

Up on my Soapbox

Up on My Soapbox: I could be wrong, but I rather doubt that a concerned owner, whose dog is experiencing skin or coat problems and who sees a food that is specifically labeled "Sensitive

141

Skin", stops and ponders: "*Well, the company does not actually state outright that this food cures sensitive skin problems. Nor do they say that they have proven that the food supports healthy skin. Therefore, I know better than to expect this food to anything at all to help my dog*".

I may be going out on a limb here, but I believe this owner is much more likely to be thinking "*Oh, look! A food that is designed to help Barney's sensitive and itchy skin! I will give it a try because poor Barney's skin has been terribly bad lately. I bet this food can help him!*". Ka-ching. Another day, another unregulated and misleading pet food health claim, another sale. Poor Barney.

Take Away for Dog Folks: If your dog is continually or excessively itchy or has skin problems, please make a visit to your veterinarian, not to your local pet supply store. It is important to obtain an accurate diagnosis for skin problems because the majority of these are *not related to food.* Rather, the most common causes of excessively itchiness in dogs are allergies to environmental allergens such as house dust mites, pollens and molds or fleas. Only after these causes have been eliminated should food be looked at as a potential underlying cause.

Cited Reference: Johnson LN, Heintze CR, Linder DE, Freeman LM. Evaluation of marketing claims, ingredients, and nutrient profiles of over-the-counter diets marketed for skin and coat health of dogs. *Journal of the American Veterinary Medical Association* 2015; 246:1334-1338.

23. Is mislabeling a problem in commercial dog foods?

By law, the ingredients in a commercial dog food must be reported on the label in descending order of preponderance by weight at the time of processing. This means that ingredients that are found first in the list are present in greatest abundance in the food. In addition to this regulation, AAFCO also provides designated ingredient terms that pet food companies must use to identify all of the ingredients that are included in their products. There are several limitations to these lists, one of which is that AAFCO specifically prohibits the inclusion of any type of descriptor regarding an ingredient's original source or its nutritional quality.

However, until recently, it was generally presumed that *listed* ingredients would actually be present in a food and that *unlisted* ingredients would not be present. Unfortunately, such a presumption may be ill-founded. Research studies published in the scientific literature over the past several years have shown that at least some brands of commercial dog foods have ingredient lists that do not always conform to what is actually *in* the food. Here are their findings:

Study 1: Four brands of dry dog food that are marketed as novel protein source foods containing venison were tested for the presence of other protein sources (1). Two of the products listed chicken and one listed rice protein in addition to venison on their label ingredient panels. ***Results:*** Of the four foods, three tested positive for the presence of soy protein and one tested positive for the presence of beef protein. In all cases, neither beef nor soy products were reported in the product's ingredient list. It is also somewhat ironic to note that one of the foods that tested positive for soy protein carried a front label claim emphatically stating, "*No Soy!*".

Study 2: The same team of researchers subsequently tested four retail dry dog foods that carried a *"No Soy"* label claim and seven therapeutic dry foods marketed to veterinarians for use in diagnosing soy allergies in dogs (2). ***Results:*** Soy protein was detected in three of the four retail brands. Of the seven veterinary-prescribed foods, four were found to contain low levels of soy protein.

Study 3: Twelve limited-ingredient diets (LIDs) and one veterinary-prescribed hydrolyzed protein product were tested for the presence of animal origin ingredients not reported on their ingredient label (3). This study used DNA analysis and microscopic analysis of food particles that allowed distinction between the tissues of mammals, fish and birds. ***Results:*** Of the 12 products, the species of animal identified by microscopic and DNA analysis matched the food label's ingredient list *in only two*. In the remaining 10 products, bone tissue fragments from one or more unreported animal source proteins were present.

Study 4: A comprehensive study published in the journal *Food Control* examined the content of 52 brands of commercial dog and cat food using DNA analysis (4). ***Results:*** Of the 52 products, 31 (60 %) had no labeling violations, meaning that the protein ingredients that were reported in the ingredient list completely matched the sources that were identified via DNA analysis. However, 21 brands (40 %) contained protein sources that were not listed on the ingredient list or in one case, a protein source that could not be identified. In three of these products, the protein source listed on the ingredient panel was *entirely absent from the food*. Chicken was the most common undeclared protein source in the mislabeled foods. This is not surprising because chicken is generally one of the least expensive animal source proteins. The presence of goat meat (yes, you read that correctly) was found in 9 products.

Study 5: Researchers tested brands of dog and cat foods that were labeled as either vegetarian or vegan (5). None of the products reported animal-based components in their ingredient list. **Results:** All six of the dry (extruded) foods that were tested contained DNA from beef, pork or sheep and five of the six contained DNA from multiple animal species. One of the 8 canned vegetarian foods contained animal DNA (beef). Similar to earlier studies that have found the DNA of undeclared meats in dog foods, the amount of animal-based ingredients in the foods could not be quantified. The researchers could not speculate whether the labeling violations were a result of deliberate adulteration or unintentional cross-contamination of vegetarian products with meat-containing foods produced at the same facility.

Take Away for Dog Folks: The authors of the first three papers wrote that their objectives were to examine limited ingredient diets for the presence of undeclared protein ingredients. Their concern was the increased use of these foods by owners and some veterinarians to diagnose food-related allergies. The scientists' concern was that owners were unwittingly using the over-the-counter limited-ingredient products as an alternative to the more expensive and supposedly better controlled veterinary-prescribed foods. The expectation was that the prescription products would contain only what their labels claimed, while the retail foods would be contaminated with other ingredients. What they found however, was that both the retail and veterinary-prescribed foods have the potential to be mislabeled (*Oops*).

Regardless of results not always showing what one expects to find, there are several important issues that this group of studies expose:

🐾 *Intentional or accidental?* The analytical tests used in these studies are able to detect very small quantities of undeclared protein sources. Therefore, a positive result does not necessarily mean that the source was contributing a large proportion of the food's protein. It only means that an undeclared protein source was present. This might occur accidentally as

145

a result of ingredient cross-contamination during transportation, via airborne particle transfer in the manufacturing plant, or through the use of equipment that was not thoroughly cleaned between production runs. Regardless of intent, these causes are still problems and should be addressed in good manufacturing practice and quality control procedures. Alternatively, the identification of chicken as the most frequently undeclared animal protein source certainly suggests the potential for intentional substitution and mislabeling, seeing that chicken is less expensive than the ingredients that it augmented or replaced.

🐾 ***Diagnosing/managing allergic dogs***: For those who live with dogs suspected of having a food allergy, these results are bad news regardless of knowing quantities or intent. Although the concentration of a food allergen that is needed to trigger an allergic response in dogs is not known, it is expected to be similar to that in people – very low. These studies suggest that feeding a veterinary-prescribed elimination diet may not be a guarantee that the dog is not exposed to a suspected allergen. In addition, feeding a dog a retail brand LID may not be an effective approach even when food allergens have been identified. For these reasons, many nutritionists now recommend feeding a homemade elimination diet for the diagnosis of food allergies in dogs. Once the allergenic protein is identified, extreme care will be needed during food selection.

🐾 ***Trust:*** Last, but certainly not least, are the issues of food mislabeling, manufacturing integrity and consumer trust. The cases in which listed ingredients were completely absent from the food and were substituted with other protein ingredients, are in clear violation of labeling regulations. What is not known is whether ingredient substitutions, additions, and mislabeling are intentional or accidental or where within the production chain these adulterations are taking place. What does seem clear however, is that consumers cannot always trust the ingredient list to represent only ingredients that are present in a product.

Up on my Soapbox

Up on My Soapbox: The Federal Food, Drug and Cosmetic Act requires that all pet foods sold in the United States are safe, produced under sanitary conditions, contain no harmful substances, and *are truthfully labeled* (emphasis mine). Perhaps I am being picky, but labeling a food as an LID, as containing a particular protein source, or as vegetarian and then not ensuring that the food indeed contains or lacks the identified ingredients, seems to qualify as not being truthful. Not only are such egregious errors in violation of both FDA and AAFCO regulations, but they seriously impact the trust that dog owners have in pet food manufacturers.

What can you do as a dog owner? First, remember that a substantial proportion of products that were tested in the studies contained all and only those protein ingredients that their labels reported. They were not mislabeled. If you feed commercial dog food, seek out reputable manufacturers. These are the producers who provide ingredient source information, manufacturing details, safety records, and detailed product information to their consumers.

If you have concerns, contact the manufacturer of the food, and ask them how they verify the integrity of their products, specifically, the ingredients that they include in their foods. If they are not forthcoming and transparent with their response, find another producer who is. The good news is that the pressure that research studies such as these place on pet food companies and upon the industry as a whole will hopefully encourage increased transparency and improved regulatory oversight – something that we are apparently in need of.

Cited Studies:

1. Raditic DM, Remillard RL, Tater KC. ELISA testing for common food antigens in four dry dog foods used in dietary elimination trials. *Journal of Animal Physiology and Animal Nutrition* 2010; 95:90-97.

2. Willis-Mahn C, Remillard R, Tater K. ELISA testing for soy antigens in dry dog foods used in dietary elimination trials. *Journal of the American Animal Hospital Association* 2014; 50:383-389.

3. Ricci R, Granato A, Vascellari M, Boscarato M, Palagiano C, Andrighetto I, Diez M, Mutinelli F. Identification of undeclared sources of animal origin in canine dry foods used in dietary elimination trials. *Journal of Animal Physiology and Animal Nutrition* 2013; 97:32-38.

4. Okuma TA, Hellberg RS. Identification of meat species in pet foods using a real-time polymerase chain reaction (PCR) assay. *Food Control* 2015; 50:9-17.

5. Kanakubo, K, Fascetti AJ, Larsen JA. Determination of mammalian deoxyribonucleic acid (DNA) in commercial vegetarian and vegan diets for dogs and cats. *Animal Physiology and Animal Nutrition* 2016; 101:70-74.

24. Should I worry about mercury levels in fish-based foods?

The concentration of mercury in fish has been a concern in human diets for a number of years. Should we extend these concerns to dog food? Let's look at what we currently know about mercury in commercial foods and how to ensure that your dog is not consuming excessive levels of this element.

What is mercury? Mercury (Hg) is a naturally occurring metal that is found everywhere; it is in the soil, in water and in the atmosphere. Terrestrial plants take in mercury from the atmosphere, while aquatic plants and microorganisms absorb it from water. Certain fish species, classified as bioaccumulators, concentrate mercury in their tissues. Species that have unusually high levels of mercury include tuna, mackerel, marlin, swordfish, and shark. Conversely, other species of fish and shellfish such as salmon, sardines, scallops, and crab contain lower levels.

Mercury is not a required mineral and is toxic to humans and other animals. Several forms exist in the environment. The organic form, methylmercury, is considered to be the most toxic because it is more readily absorbed into the body compared to other forms. Methylmercury is the form that predominates in the fish meals that are used in pet foods. However, its bioavailability (i.e., the proportion that a dog absorbs) from pet foods has not been measured and is not known.

What we *do* know is that a dose of 500 micrograms of methylmercury per day is acutely toxic to dogs, leading to rapid illness and death. Clinical signs of mercury poisoning include gastrointestinal ulcerations and hemorrhaging, kidney damage, and neurological damage. Because mercury accumulates in tissues, chronic effects of lower levels of consumption over long periods of time can occur.

149

No Safe Upper Limit for Dogs: There is no question that excessive levels of mercury should *not* be present in the foods that we feed to our dogs. Unfortunately, a safe upper limit in pet foods has not been established by either the Association of American Feed Control Officials (AAFCO) or the National Research Council (NRC). Nor does there exist a compulsory requirement for pet food companies to test their products for mercury (or any other heavy metal). In Europe, the European Commission Directive (ECD) has set a maximum level of total mercury at 400 micrograms per kilogram of food for dry dog foods (12 percent moisture). However, this concentration appears to be somewhat arbitrary as there is no empirical evidence that supports setting this level.

How Much Mercury is in Dog Foods? In recent years, several groups of researchers, from separate institutions, have examined this question and have published studies that report mercury levels in commercial pet foods. Here is a summary of their findings:

- 🐾 *Study 1 (2011):* This paper was produced by a group of mineral scientists (1). They examined the heavy metal content of 58 brands of dog and cat food and published a comprehensive report that included comparisons of the mercury levels that they found in pet foods to recommended maximum levels in human foods. Cat foods had higher mercury contents than dog foods, but none of the foods exceeded 100 micrograms/kilogram of food. The highest level in a dog food was 26.8 micrograms/kg, found in a dry dog food. This is well below the maximum set by the ECD.

- 🐾 *Study 2 (2016):* Two researchers with the Department of Natural Resources and Environmental Science at the University of Nevada measured mercury concentrations in 54 brands of dog food and 47 brands of cat food (2). The tested foods had mercury concentrations ranging between 1.0 and *over 600 micrograms/kilogram* of food. Foods with the highest concentrations (>100 micrograms/kg) were primarily canned cat foods that contained fish as the primary protein source. The highest reported concentration for a dog food was about 60 micrograms/kg which is substantially lower than the maximum established for European pet foods of 400 micrograms/kg.

🐾 *Study 3 (2018):* Joseph Wakshlag and a group of researchers at Cornell University tested 51 dry dog foods (3). They divided the foods into three categories, based upon the primary protein source in the food. Fish-containing dog foods contained significantly higher levels of mercury when compared to poultry and red meat-containing foods. In this study, the researchers reported mercury levels on an energy basis, rather than on a weight basis. When compared with human consumption patterns, the authors reported that dogs consuming the median range of mercury in fish-based foods would be consuming *5 times the maximum recommended levels of mercury for humans* (see below).

🐾 *Study 4 (2019):* Last, researchers at the University of California measured the elemental mercury and methylmercury content in 24 commercial dog foods (4). In contrast to previous studies that detected mercury in almost all sampled foods, this paper reported that mercury was non-detectable in 21 out of the 24 samples that were tested. Of the three foods that were found to contain mercury, one food contained *490 micrograms/kilogram of food*, a level that exceeds the maximum established for European pet foods.

Let's Do Some Math: The Environmental Protection Agency (EPA) currently recommends that an adult human should consume no more than 0.1 micrograms of mercury per kilogram of body weight per day. If we apply this recommendation to a person who weighs 175 lbs., this is equivalent to 8 micrograms of mercury per day, as the maximum safe level.

Now let's compare this number to several of the reported values for dog foods. As our example dog, I will use a 36-lb (16.4 kg), young, adult dog who has an estimated caloric requirement of 1000 kilocalories (kcals) per day. We will assume that this dog is consuming a dry food that contains 4000 kilocalories per kilogram (about an average adult maintenance food). On a weight basis, he would need 250 grams of food per day to meet his energy needs. To make this a bit more personal, let's call this fellow Stanley.

Hi! I'm Stanley!

For each of the four papers that are summarized above, I selected the food that had the highest reported level of mercury and calculated the number of micrograms of mercury that Stanley would ingest daily if fed that food (Note: The papers reported mercury in several different ways [units], which required slightly different calculations for each situation):

Study 1: The highest concentration of mercury in this study was 26.8 microgram/kg of food. If fed this food exclusively, Stanley would ingest **6.7 micrograms of mercury per day**.

Study 2: The highest concentration of mercury in this paper was 60 micrograms/kg of food. If fed this food exclusively, Stanley would ingest **15.0 micrograms of mercury per day**.

Study 3: The highest concentration of mercury in this study was 13.9 micrograms/1000 kcals. Stanley would ingest **13.9 micrograms of mercury per day**.

Study 4: The highest concentration of mercury in this study was 490 micrograms/kg of food. Stanley would ingest **122.5 micrograms of mercury per day**.

In three of these four examples, based upon actual foods, Stanley would be ingesting more than the EPA upper recommended limit of mercury (8.0 micrograms per day) for a human subject weighing 175 lbs. (not to put too fine a point on this, but a human who is almost 5-times Stanley's weight).

Up on my Soapbox

On My Soapbox: Collectively, these studies suggest that the levels of mercury in most commercial pet foods is very low and will not put dogs at risk. However, a small number of foods had higher than expected concentrations of mercury. These levels were usually found in fish-based foods. For each of the four papers reported above, I selected the food that contained the highest level of mercury and calculated how much mercury Stanley would ingest if he was fed that food exclusively.

These calculations revealed that, in three of the four foods, levels exceeded the upper limit set by the EPA for a human subject. Although these concentrations were always much lower than the levels known to be acutely toxic to dogs, it is important to note that we do not know what level of mercury is safe for ·dogs over long periods of time (chronic consumption).

Here are the Current Facts:

🐾 A safe upper limit for mercury in dog foods is not known.

🐾 There is no mandatory requirement that companies test their products for mercury, even when fish is a primary ingredient.

🐾 Some foods (albeit a small number) contain levels of mercury that, if fed exclusively, would result in a dog consuming daily levels of mercury that exceed recommended EPA limits for humans.

On a practical level, a reasonable approach is to avoid feeding only foods that contain fish as the primary protein source as a dog's singular food source. These data provide additional support for the recommendation to avoid feeding a single brand of food to dogs over long periods of time. It is time to robustly reject the outdated advice that dogs do best when fed one brand of food for their entire lives. Just as humans are advised to avoid frequent consumption of tuna because of the risk of excessive mercury exposure, so too is it prudent to avoid feeding dogs a single fish-based food, given that we do not have good information regarding mercury levels in all foods.

If you are concerned about mercury levels in the food or foods that you feed to your dog, contact the manufacturer and inquire if they are testing for mercury and other heavy metals. Although there is no reason to panic, the data presented in these studies do inform us that mercury levels may be too high in a small number of commercial pet foods.

Cited Studies:

1. Atkins P, Ernyei L, Driscoll W, et al. Analysis of toxic trace metals in pet foods using cryogenic grinding and quantification by IPC-MS, Parts 1 and 2. *Spectroscopy* 2011; 26:46-56; 57-68.

2. Luippold A and Sexauer GM. Mercury concentrations in wet and dry cat and dog food. *Animal Feed Science and Technology* 2016; 222: 190-193.

3. Kim HT, Loftus JP, Mann S, Wakshlag JJ. Evaluation of arsenic, cadmium, lead, and mercury contamination in over-the-counter available dry dog foods with different animal ingredients (red meat, poultry, and fish). *Frontiers in Veterinary Science* 2018: October, doi: 10.3389/fvets.2018.00264.

4. Sires RA, Fascetti AJ, Puschner B. Determination of total mercury and methylmercury concentrations in commercial canine diets. *Topics in Companion Animal Medicine* 2019; 6-10; doi.org/10.1053/j.tcam.2019.02.002

25. Are there health benefits to feeding raw?

Raw feeding has increased markedly in popularity in recent years. While still making up a small portion of the pet food market, raw foods are definitely here to stay. Moreover, perhaps more so than any other type of feeding regimen, dog owners who feed raw are highly dedicated to this form of feeding.

There are several options for owners who choose to feed raw. These include using a homemade recipe, purchasing a base mix that can be added to raw meat, or buying a frozen or freeze-dried complete and balanced product. For all of these forms, many health and wellness claims are made. The table below summarizes some of the most common of these.

CLAIMED HEALTH BENEFITS OF RAW FEEDING
❀ Improved overall health and vitality
❀ Better digestion and fecal (stool) quality
❀ Improvements in coat and skin health
❀ Cleaner teeth and healthy gums
❀ Enhanced gut (gastrointestinal) health
❀ Increased energy and muscle strength
❀ Reduced risk of obesity
❀ Enhanced immune function and reduced cancer risk
❀ Increased # of "Swipe Rights" on Tinder photo profile

Okay, the last one may be an exaggeration. Everyone knows that most dogs prefer Match.

Is There Evidence? Despite strong belief by some raw feeders in these benefits, there are few studies that provide any scientific evidence to support them. We do have a bit of evidence from research conducted by a group of nutritionists at the University of Illinois (1). Their study compared the effects of feeding a raw diet to three types of cooked and processed foods.

The Study: A group of eight adult dogs were fed four foods on a rotating basis. Each food was fed for 28 days. The researchers measured intake, feces quality, body weight/condition, and food digestibility. As a general measure of health, they collected blood samples for serum chemistry measurements. The four foods that were studied were:

- 🐾 **Dry (extruded) food**
- 🐾 **Raw food**
- 🐾 **Moderately cooked, fresh**
- 🐾 **Moderately cooked, fresh, grain-free**

Results: The foods were all well accepted, and the dogs remained healthy throughout the study period. Food comparison results found the following:

- 🐾 *Total (dry matter) digestibility*: There were no significant differences in dry matter (total) digestibility among the four products. Digestibility coefficients ranged between 82.6 % [dry food] and 85.1 % [moderately cooked, grain-free]. The digestibility coefficient for the raw food was 83.6 %. The raw diet was not more digestible than either the extruded food or the two moderately cooked foods. These digestibility values are considered to be moderate – not rock stars, but not poor quality, either.

- 🐾 *Protein digestibility*: There were significant differences in protein digestibility among the foods. Protein digestibility of the moderately cooked, grain-free food was significantly higher (94.6 %) than the protein digestibility of the raw food

(88.3 %) or the extruded food (85.1 %). The coefficient for the raw food was a bit lower than the researchers expected based upon previous work. However, a value of 88 % is still a respectable value and considered to be highly digestible.

- **Poop quantity**: Total fecal output (yes, researchers measure these things) was *highest* when the dogs were being fed the raw diet and lowest when the dogs were consuming the moderately cooked, grain-free food. This difference was substantial – more than 100 grams per day when fed raw compared with 52 grams per day when fed the cooked food. The difference became less dramatic when expressed as either dry matter or a proportion of intake. However, the raw food continued to produce more fecal matter than the other three products.

- **Poop quality**: All of the foods resulted in acceptable fecal quality. However, when fed the raw product, dogs produced feces that were softer than those produced when being fed any of the other three foods. Their feces were still considered within the normal range of "firmness" however. Feeding the moderately cooked food resulted in significantly higher fecal concentrations of two by-products of large intestinal protein fermentation – indole and phenol. The cause or health significance of this is not completely understood, but these two compounds are one source of "stinky poops" that owners may complain about.

- **Gut microbes**: All four of the products caused modifications in the intestinal microbiota. When dogs were consuming the raw or the moderately cooked, grain-free diets, overall microbial population diversity was reduced compared to when they were consuming the extruded food. Fecal microbial shifts that occurred in response to the raw or moderately cooked foods, which were high in protein and fat, were similar to the shifts that have been reported in human subjects consuming high-protein/high-fat diets. The researchers not-

158

ed that these shifts – reduced species diversity, increased Fusobacteria and Proteobacteria, and decreased Actinobacteria – agree with other reports of the effect of a raw diet on the dog's gut microbiome (2,3,4). While this shift is generally considered to be negative in terms of health, all of the dogs in this study and others remained healthy while consuming the test diets. Therefore, the long-term effects of these changes are not known and require further study.

☙ *Overall health*: The dogs in this study remained healthy, had blood chemistry values within normal ranges, and showed normal activity levels. All of the products were well accepted and readily consumed. It is worth noting that more calories (kcal) per day were consumed when dogs were fed the raw food compared with when they were fed the extruded diet (1202 kcal/day vs. 806 kcal/day). This difference probably reflects the high palatability of the raw diet but also suggests that overconsumption of calories may have developed over long-term feeding of the raw food.

Take Away for Dog Folks: This study found that dogs accepted all three types of foods – extruded dry, moderately cooked, and raw – and remained healthy. Contrary to expectations (and claims), the raw food that was tested in this study was not significantly more digestible and did not result in less defecation or produce better quality feces. Although all four foods altered gut microbial populations, the shifts caused by the raw food are generally considered to be negative changes rather than positive. However, the complexity of the gut microbiome coupled with numerous factors that affect gut health prevent any conclusions about these changes.

So, where do we now stand with the claims box, shown previously? Here you go:

CLAIMED HEALTH BENEFITS OF RAW FEEDING	
❧ Improved overall health and vitality	No support
❧ Better digestion and fecal (stool) quality	No support
❧ Improvements in coat and skin health	Not tested
❧ Cleaner teeth and healthy gums	Not tested
❧ Enhanced gut (gastrointestinal) health	Unclear
❧ Increased energy and muscle strength	No support
❧ Reduced risk of obesity	Unclear
❧ Enhanced immune function and reduced cancer risk	Not tested
❧ Increased # of "Swipe Rights" on Tinder photo profile	Not tested (yet)

A Few Important Points:

❧ This study tested four commercial foods. All of the products are mass-marketed pet foods that are sold in supermarkets and are generally considered to be low to moderate in price point.

❧ We can only make conclusions about *these* foods – this is why the chart above states "no support" rather than "disproven". The results of this study are based upon the foods that were compared and suggest that, given the information that we now have, certain blanket claims about raw foods are not currently supported. Clearly, this cannot and should not be extrapolated to all raw diets or all dry foods.

160

🐾 Still……these results ARE important because they show that a dry food performed similarly to a raw and a moderately cooked food. It is quite probable that this has more to do with the type and quality of the starting ingredients that were used in these products much more than it has to do with raw versus cooked. By AAFCO definition, the term "chicken" can (and usually does) refer to chicken carcasses that remain after the removal of chicken meat for human consumption. These carcasses may either be processed into chicken meals for use in extruded foods or ground up and used in raw or moderately cooked foods. Same stuff, different processing.

🐾 Last – The moderately cooked foods performed every bit as well as the raw food in most measures and a bit better on some. These data suggest that perceived benefits of feeding a raw diet over a diet that has been cooked at moderate temperatures are not supported. The results also suggest that there is nothing magical about making sure that a food is RAW. Rather, it is probably more important to consider the source and quality of the starting ingredients, the degree and severity of processing, and the nutrient content of the food.

Cited Studies:

1. Algya KM, Cross T-WL, Leuck KN, Kastner ME, Baba T, Lye L, de Godoy MRC, Swanson KS. Apparent total-tract macronutrient digestibility, serum chemistry, urinalysis, and fecal characteristics, metabolites and microbiota of adult dogs fed extruded, mildly cooked, and raw diets. *Journal of Animal Science* 2018; 96:3670-3683.

2. Beloshapka AN, Dowd SE, Duclos L, Swanson KS. Comparison of fecal microbial communities of healthy adult dogs fed raw meat-based or extruded diets using 454 pyrosequencing. *Journal of Animal Science* 2011; 89; E-suppl: 284.

3. Sandri MS, Dal Monego G, Conte S, Sgorlon B, Stefon B. Raw meat-based diet influences fecal microbiome and end products of fermentation in healthy dogs. *BMC Veterinary Research* 2017; 13:65.

4. Bermingham EN, Maclean P, Thaoma DG, Cave NJ, Young W. Key bacterial families (*Clostridiaceae, Erysipelotrichaceae and Bacteroidaceae*) are related to the digestion of protein and energy in dogs. *Peer J 5:e3019 https://doi.org/10.7717/peerj.3019*

26. Are raw diets safe to feed to dogs?

A primary concern that veterinarians and some other pet professionals have about feeding raw foods to dogs is safety. Specifically, the question is whether or not raw pet foods are more likely
to be contaminated with pathogenic bacteria when compared to
cooked foods. As with all things Science Dog, we look to science
and evidence for answers to this question. Several studies have
examined the prevalence of bacterial and parasitic contamination in commercially produced raw dog foods. This chapter provides a summary of their findings.

Study 1: Dutch epidemiologists with the Division of Veterinary
Public Health in Utrecht, Netherlands tested a group of 35 commercial raw, meat-based diets for the presence of bacterial and
parasitic pathogens (1). The researchers purposely selected
popular brands sold by retailers. All of the samples were stored
according to label recommendations prior to analysis.

🐾 *Results:* The pathogenic bacteria species *Escherichia coli* was
found in 30 products (86%). The majority of the contaminated foods (28 products) contained an antibiotic-resistant
strain of this microbe and eight were contaminated with a
strain that causes serious illness in humans. *Listeria* species
were found in 43% and *Salmonella* species were found in
20% of the tested foods. Several products were contaminated
with parasites, but this risk was substantially lower than that
of bacterial contamination.

🐾 *Conclusions:* Because several of the pathogens that were isolated were zoonotic (i.e., pathogenic to humans) and because
the transmission of antibiotic-resistant bacterial strains is an
increasingly serious public health issue, the authors conclude
that pet owners should be informed of the potential health

risks (to humans and to pets) associated with feeding raw, meat-based diets.

Study 2: Although conducted in cats rather than dogs, this paper is important because it examines the effects of feeding a raw diet on changes in fecal bacterial populations and the potential for exposure to antibiotic-resistant microbes (2). The study enrolled 17 pet cats that were fed dry, extruded cat food (the control group), and 19 cats that were fed a frozen or fresh raw diet. Fecal samples were collected weekly and were analyzed for the presence of antibiotic-resistant forms of species within the family of *Enterobacteriaceae*. In addition, 53 cat foods (18 raw products and 35 dry or canned products) were analyzed for the presence of the same bacteria.

🐾 ***Results:*** In the control group, three of 51 fecal samples (5.9%) were positive for the presence of antibiotic-resistant microbes. In the raw-fed group of cats, 37 of 57 fecal samples (65%) were positive for antibiotic-resistant bacteria. When present, the concentration of these microbes was also found to be significantly higher in cats fed raw diets. Finally, 77.8 % of the raw foods and 0 % (none) of the cooked foods were found to be contaminated with antibiotic-resistant bacteria.

🐾 ***Conclusions:*** This study found a strong association between feeding cats a raw diet and fecal shedding of antibiotic-resistant bacteria. This association suggests a substantial risk of transmission of antibiotic-resistant bacteria to both the animals and to the owners who handle these foods and who may also be exposed to their cat's fecal matter.

Study 3: In this paper, samples of 60 commercially available, frozen raw foods were tested for microbial contamination (3).

🐾 ***Results:*** Bacteria of the taxonomic family *Enterobacteriaceae* were found in all 60 samples (100 %). In half of these (52 %), the concentration exceeded the threshold level considered acceptable by EU regulations. *Clostridium perfringens* was detected in 18 brands (30 %) and concentrations exceeded the maximum allowed in two brands. *Salmonella* species were found in 4 samples and *Campylobacter* species were isolated in three samples.

🐾 *Conclusions:* Like other authors, the researchers recommend that pet owners are informed about the pathogen risks associated with raw feeding. They also go a bit further, stating that in view of the antibiotic-resistance problem, dogs who are being treated with antimicrobials should not be fed raw diets; nor should dogs living in homes with infants, elderly people, or immunocompromised individuals because these subgroups are more vulnerable to infection.

Review Study: In this systematic review, the authors examine mor than 30 independent scientific studies that measured bacterial pathogens in raw pet foods (4). In both Europe and the United States, a high proportion of the tested foods had contamination levels that exceeded the minimum acceptable levels for human meat products. The most common pathogens that were found were *Salmonella* species and *Escherichia coli*. Recent papers reported antimicrobial-resistant forms of several different bacterial species.

🐾 *Conclusions:* The authors conclude that there remains little doubt, based upon the published evidence, that the prevalence of potentially serious pathogens is substantially higher in raw pet food than in heat-treated foods and that these levels may pose a significant health risk to both pets and humans.

Take Away for Dog Folks: Here is a summary of the scientific evidence that we currently have regarding benefits and risks associated with feeding raw diets:

❧ *Health benefits?* As with any broad category of feeding, the long-term health benefits of feeding raw foods to dogs is difficult to study. To date, most of the purported advantages of feeding raw are based on personal stories and anecdotes and do not have support from controlled feeding trials. The few feeding trials that have examined general health have reported that dogs fed a nutritionally balanced raw diet remain healthy but have not demonstrated enhanced health benefits above those of dogs fed other foods. This does not mean that there are no benefits; it simply means that we do not know and that the numerous health claims for raw foods are not based on scientific evidence (see Chapter 25 for details).

❧ *Improved digestibility?* Some owners select a raw food for their dog because they are interested in feeding less highly processed foods. In the dog food realm, both dry, extruded food (kibble) and canned foods are highly processed and are almost exclusively produced from feed grade (i.e. "inedible") ingredients. The way in which these ingredients are handled and cooked during processing causes moderate to severe changes in protein quality and the loss of some nutrients. Therefore, it is not surprising to find that raw diets are often higher in digestibility than more highly processed foods. However, digestibility and nutrient availability are also influenced by the quality of the starting ingredients, as discussed in Section 3 (more about this in Chapter 31).

❧ *Safety?* The studies reported in this chapter provide evidence that commercial raw pet foods are more likely to be contaminated with bacterial pathogens and with strains of these pathogens that are resistant to antibiotics than are heat-treated products. These results show that dogs and people may be at risk of infection and that these foods are a potential vector for the spread of antibiotic-resistant strains of bacteria to other animals and people.

If you are a raw feeder, you can respond to this information in an informed manner. Ask producers about their methods for controlling bacterial contamination (see Chapters 28 and 29), quality control measures, and their company's recall history. Select foods that have been shown to be free of pathogenic bacteria and have not been recalled. When feeding your dog, avoid handling raw products, wash your hands and food preparation surfaces thoroughly, and monitor your dog carefully for signs of illness or gastrointestinal infection.

Cited Studies:

1. van Bree FPJ, Bokken G, Mineur R, et al. Zoonotic bacteria and parasites found in raw meat-based diets for cats and dogs. *Veterinary Record* 2018; 183:50-58.

2. Baede VO, Broens EM, Spaninks MR, et al. Raw pet food as a risk factor for shedding extended-spectrum beta-lactamase producing *Enterobacteriaceiae* in household cats. *PLoS One* 2017; November: doi.org/10.1371/journal.pone.0187239.

3. Hellgren J, Hasto LS, Wikstrom C, Fernstrom LL, Hansson I. Occurrence of *Salmonella, Campylobacter, Clostridium* and *Enterobacteriaceae* in raw meat-based diets for dogs. *Veterinary Record* 2019; 184:442-450.

4. Davies Rh, Lawes JR, Wales AD. Raw diets for dogs and cats: A review, with particular reference to microbiological hazards. *Journal of Small Animal Practice* 2019; 60:329-339.

27. Does freezing raw food prevent contamination?

Raw dog foods come in several forms. One of the most common is as frozen rolls or patties. Following purchase, pet owners store these foods in their freezer and portions are removed, thawed, and fed on a daily basis.

Reportedly, the intent of keeping raw foods frozen is to minimize or completely eliminate the risk of microbial growth and transmission. It is believed (and often stated by raw food proponents) that freezing these products prevents the growth of microbes that may be present, thereby reducing or completely eliminating the risk of transmission of food-borne pathogens to dogs and people.

But do we know these beliefs to be true? Is there evidence supporting the oft-stated claim that keeping a raw dog food frozen or refrigerated prevents food pathogens from proliferating? Luckily, we have a bit of science to help us to answer this question.

The Study: A group of food scientists evaluated the microbial quality of commercially available raw dog foods sold on-line and shipped in a frozen state to consumers (1). A set of 29 raw dog foods, containing a variety of meat ingredients, were obtained from three different on-line companies. All of the foods were delivered in a frozen state and were immediately placed into a freezer. Following 24 hours of storage, samples were thawed at refrigerator temperature (2 C/36 F) for approximately 15 hours and were sampled for microbial analysis. Following the initial sampling, foods were stored at either proper refrigerator temperature (2 C/36 F) or at a slightly higher temperature (7 C/45 F) and were resampled again after 24, 48 and 72 hours.

Results: Well, some bugs were found:

🐾 *Time zero:* Significant and potentially harmful numbers of pathogenic bacteria were found in a majority of the foods when they were tested *immediately* after thawing. Of the 29 products, 19 had total bacterial counts at time 0 that exceeded the maximum level allowed for meats intended for human consumption. In addition, the counts for *Escherichia coli* were unacceptably high in almost all of the foods (26/29).

🐾 *Refrigerated samples:* Unsurprisingly, microbial loads increased significantly over the three-day storage period, *even when stored properly at refrigerator temperatures.* These findings led the researchers to recommend always feeding food portions on the same day that they are thawed and to avoid storing thawed raw dog foods in the refrigerator, even for short periods of time.

🐾 *Temperature matters:* Storing foods at 7 degrees C (45 degrees F) resulted in much higher bacterial counts and higher levels of contamination with zoonotic microbial species than did storing the foods at the proper refrigerator temperature of 2 C/36 F (again, not surprising).

🐾 *Freezing myths:* The researchers conclude that the microbial quality of commercial frozen raw dog foods appears to be poor and carries considerable risk of contamination with zoonotic bacteria. Moreover, these bacteria *are* present at the time of thawing/feeding and proliferate rapidly with storage, even at proper refrigerator temperatures.

Take Away for Dog Folks: This is not good news, either for the dogs being fed these products or for the owners who are handling them. That said, these results should not be tremendously surprising, given what we learned in the previous chapter. What is unique to this study is the examination of microbial contamination to frozen foods immediately following thawing and during short-term storage.

169

The researchers stored the thawed foods at both normal refrigerator temperatures and at temperatures that were slightly higher than normal during the 3-day storage period. They used this approach because time/temperature transgressions due to consumer food mishandling are reported to be common contributing factors to outbreaks of foodborne illnesses in humans.

Therefore, it is not unreasonable to assume that breaches in food handling practices occur similarly when dog owners feed raw foods to their dogs. Considering the high *initial* microbial loads found in many of the foods in this study, coupled with the very rapid increase in microbial numbers during both proper and improper storage, it is clear that owners should take particular care when handling, storing and feeding frozen raw foods to their dogs.

Cited Study:

1. Morelli G, Catellani P, Scapin RM, et al. Evaluation of microbial contamination and effects of storage in raw meat-based dog foods purchased on-line. *Journal of Animal Physiology and Animal Nutrition* 2020; 104:690-697.

28. Is freeze-dried raw food safer than other forms?

The two previous chapters address what we currently understand regarding the contamination risks associated with feeding raw food diets to dogs. To date, the science that is available tells us this:

1. The prevalence of potentially serious microbial pathogens is substantially higher in raw pet foods than in heat-treated foods (see Chapter 26).

2. The belief that *freezing* a raw dog food kills food pathogens or reduces microbial contamination is not supported by evidence (see Chapter 27).

So, what about some of the other forms of raw diets for dogs, for example, freeze-dried products?

Freeze-dried Raw Dog Food

What is Freeze-Drying? Freeze-dry processing is a common type of water removal process that is used to preserve commercial raw pet foods. It involves a three-step process in which the formulated food is first frozen and then exposed to a strong vacuum as the temperature is raised slightly. This causes the frozen water in the food to sublimate, which means that it goes straight from ice to vapor, skipping the liquid phase.

Low Moisture Products: Of all food processing methods that are currently used for pet foods, freeze-drying results in the lowest level of moisture remaining in the product – *only 2 to 5 percent.* Similar to other "gentle" processing approaches such as air-drying and dehydration, freeze drying is claimed to preserve more of the nutritional content of foods and to reduce the loss of essential nutrients and damage to food proteins that is associated with traditional heat treatments such as extrusion and canning. While a reasonable belief, studies with pet foods that support this supposition are still lacking.

What about Microbial Contamination? There is, however, a study that has compared the presence of microbial contamination in commercially produced freeze-dried dog foods with levels in frozen products (1). Although small in scope, this paper provides needed insight regarding the question of whether or not the freeze-drying process helps to protect raw dog foods from microbial contamination.

The Study: The researchers sampled 15 different frozen raw foods and two freeze-dried raw foods. Samples were collected by purchasing foods from both physical (brick and mortar) stores and through on-line pet supply services. The types of meats found in the products included chicken, duck, fish, and beef. Measurement of bacterial counts took place immediately following thawing the frozen products and rehydrating the freeze-dried products per package instructions.

Results: The researchers found the following differences:

🐾 *Food type:* Fourteen of the 15 frozen food samples (93 %) had Total Bacterial Counts (TBC) that exceeded acceptable

172

standard limits set for foods and food containers. In contrast, both of the freeze-dried products that were tested had counts that were lower than the allowed limits, interpreted to mean that these would not be considered to be contaminated products.

🐾 *Bacterial species:* The most common microbial species identified were *Salmonella* (9 foods), *Listeria* (9 foods), *Escherichia coli* (7 foods), and *Staphylococcus aureus* (7 foods). These results are consistent with other reports of microbial contamination in raw pet foods (see Chapter 26 and Chapter 27).

🐾 *Meat type:* Foods that were chicken-based were significantly more likely to be contaminated with *Staphylococcus aureus* and *Listeria* when compared to other meat forms (beef or fish). However, given the small number of samples tested in this study, this may not be a reliable finding.

Take Away for Dog Folks: This study can be viewed as a bit more evidence to add to the growing body that we have regarding the safety of raw food diets for dogs. The finding that frozen raw foods had high levels of bacterial contamination should not be surprising at this point. At question is not whether raw food diets are more likely to be contaminated with microbial pathogens (evidence shows that they are, and that freezing does not matter), but rather how owners can choose wisely to minimize risk of transmission to both dogs and humans.

Reducing the water content of a food product is a well-accepted approach to preserving foods and is used in the preparation of both human and pet food products. The very low moisture content of freeze-dried raw dog foods appears, at least in the two foods studied here, to significantly reduce the survival of food-borne pathogens at the point of feeding. So, if you feed raw or are considering feeding raw, these results may be helpful as you examine the various options and types of foods that are available.

Cited Study:

1. Kananub S, Pinniam N, Phothitheerabut S, Krajanglikit P. Contamination factors associated with surviving bacterial in Thai commercial raw pet foods. *Veterinary World* 2020; 13: 1988-1991.

29. What is HPP and should it be used with raw products?

High pressure processing (HPP), also called high pressure pasteurization or cold pasteurization, is a food processing technique that has been used in the human food industry for years. Products that are routinely treated with HPP include ready-to-eat meats and meals, fruit juices, packaged dips, and jams and jellies.

For dogs – if you feed a commercial raw dog food, there is now a reasonable chance that your dog is also consuming an HPP-treated product. Since passing of the Food Safety and Modernization Act (FSMA) in 2011, many raw food producers have started to use HPP to ensure compliance with the act's zero tolerance requirement regarding *Salmonella* contamination. HPP is not required of raw food manufacturers, but rather, it provides a viable means of increasing food safety without the need for heat treatment or irradiation.

What Exactly *is* HPP? High pressure processing is a non-thermal, high pressure food processing treatment. It is used to preserve products that are not destined to be heat treated to temperatures that would normally kill potentially pathogenic microbes. In the pet food industry, HPP may be used with raw (frozen), freeze-dried, and most recently, fresh-frozen/gently cooked foods. In addition to reducing a product's bacterial load, HPP also functions to increase the shelf life of treated foods.

The actual process involves applying high pressure, typically around 6,000 bar, to a packaged and sealed food submerged in a water tank. Pressure is applied for several minutes, which causes irreparable damage to the cell walls of any contaminating microbes in the product. Organisms that are most sensitive to pressure are molds, yeast and parasites, while bacteria require higher levels of pressure for inactivation. Currently, both the Food

175

and Drug Administration (FDA) and the United States Department of Agriculture (USDA) identify HPP as the preferred method for ensuring food safety in raw pet foods.

Research Studies with Dog Foods: Although HPP is used by a number of pet food companies, surprisingly little research has been conducted to study its actual effect on raw pet foods. Two questions are of interest:

1. Does HPP reduce or eliminate microbial numbers and improve the safety of raw foods?

2. Does HPP alter the nutritional value of raw foods?

Although we certainly need more research, there are three published studies that provide a few answers for dog owners (1,2,3).

HPP and Pathogen Reduction: In 2016, a group of food science researchers tested the effectiveness of HPP for reducing the microbial load in a beef-based raw dog food (1). Samples of raw food were inoculated with a non-pathogenic bacterial test species. This approach had been previously validated as a reliable method for estimating the response of pathogenic *Salmonella* contamination in foods. The product was packaged into rolls, which were then treated with a standard HPP protocol. Following treatment, samples were tested for microbial levels at 24 hours post-HPP and following 5 days of frozen storage.

Results: The results provide some good news for raw food feeders:

🐾 *Reduction in microbial contamination:* The HPP processing significantly reduced surviving numbers of microbes in the treated food. Interestingly, freezing and storing the food for 5 days prior to testing resulted in *additional* microbial deaths and even lower numbers of viable bacteria. This suggests that bacterial cells were damaged during HPP, causing cellu-

176

lar injury that led to continued bacterial destruction during freezing and storage. It is of note that more than *90 percent* of the samples had microbial levels that were less than the lowest detectable level.

🐾 ***Total death not achieved***: However, unlike some forms of food processing that completely eliminate all pathogens, essentially sterilizing the product, HPP does not appear to achieve total death or sterilization of foods. This result is of some concern given the zero-tolerance standard that food companies are currently required to meet by FSMA.

HPP and Nutritional Integrity: A concern that some raw food proponents have about HPP is that it will alter the nutritional integrity of the food. Specific worries focus on the effects of HPP on the quality of the food and on the food's protein.

Two research studies have examined these issues. The first was a feeding study in which digestibility values were measured in dogs fed either a commercial dry dog food or an HPP-treated raw food. The second was an in vitro (laboratory) study that measured changes in chicken digestibility when subjected to thermal (heat) treatment versus HPP treatment.

Feeding Study: In this study, digestibility values of a dry, extruded food and a raw food treated with HPP were compared when fed to a group of 10 healthy adult dogs (2). A disclaimer – This was *not* a well-controlled study. The study design had a few issues and the two foods differed in multiple ways, not just in the type of preservation method that was used. However, it *is* a feeding study of a raw food treated with HPP, which we need.

Results: The digestibility coefficient (%) of the dry food was very low (less than 60 percent), while the digestibility value of the HPP-treated raw food was very high (greater than 90 percent – a rock star value). This difference may have had numerous causes, so we cannot make conclusions in terms of comparing the two foods. What we *can* say however, is that in this study, the raw dog food that was treated with HPP had a very high digestibility coefficient when fed to dogs.

In Vitro Study: This study used a validated laboratory method to measure the digestibility values of chicken meat that was treated with different preservation methods (3). These included thermal processing at three different temperatures, HPP treatment, and two other non-thermal treatments.

Results: Thermal processing of chicken meat led to decreased protein digestibility values that were inversely related to cooking temperature and cooking time. As temperatures and duration increased, protein digestibility decreased. This change was dramatic; ~ 86 % protein digestibility for raw chicken compared with 65 % protein digestibility in chicken treated at the highest temperature for the longest time. These results were interpreted to reflect increased protein damage with higher heat treatment. In contrast, the protein digestibility of HPP-treated chicken meat remained high and did not differ significantly from the digestibility of raw chicken meat (86 % compared with 84 %). These results indicate that the nutritional value of chicken meat was well maintained when HPP was used but decreased when thermal processing was used.

Take Away for Dog Folks: So, for dog owners who choose to feed a raw diet, the results of these three studies suggest that:

1. HPP is an effective processing treatment that significantly reduces (though it does not completely eliminate) a raw food's bacterial load.

2. HPP-treated raw foods retain a high level of nutrient (protein and dry matter) availability.

Given the information that we currently have, a practical and evidence-based recommendation to those who wish to feed a raw food is to select products only from manufacturers who are using high pressure pasteurization as their product preservation method.

Cited Studies:

1. Hasty J, Woerner DR, Martin JN, et al. The use of high-pressure processing as a pathogen reduction tool in raw pet food. *Meat and Muscle Biology* 2016; 1(2)119.

2. Neshovska H, Shindarska Z. Comparative study of the digestibility of dry and raw food in dogs. *International Journal of Veterinary Sciences and Animal Husbandry* 2021; 6:(2):01-03.

3. Kim H, Jung AH, Park SH, et al. In vitro protein disappearance of raw chicken in dog foods decreased by thermal processing but was unaffected by non-thermal processing. *Animals* 2021, 11;1256. doi.org/10.3390/ani11051256.

30. Do human-grade & pet-grade foods differ?

In the world of commercial dog foods, the phrase "*human-grade*" is a bit of an oddity. The oddness occurs because while this term is in use on pet food labels and in marketing materials, it actually has no legal definition. Rather, the regulated terms that are used to delineate between foods that are sold for human consumption and those that are intended for consumption by pets are "*edible*" (humans can eat) and "*inedible*" (animals can eat). Still, when you see the words human-grade on a dog food package, these words *do* have important meaning and should be given careful consideration.

What IS the Difference? The distinction is an important one. Foods in the first category (*edible*) are handled, processed, transported, and stored under an entire set of regulations that are specifically designed to keep products both nutritious and safe for humans to consume. Conversely, foods in the second category (the *inedibles*, if you will) enter a separate supply stream that is demonstrably more relaxed in its requirements for preserving nutrient value and preventing microbial contamination during handling and transport. In a nutshell:

🐾 *Edible* = Highly regulated; safe for people to consume as food; ends up in your supermarket.

🐾 *Inedible* = Less intensely regulated; not considered safe for humans to consume; ends up in pet foods.

For obvious reasons, the terms edible and inedible, while technically correct, do not sit well with most dog owners.

Enter the term *"human-grade."* Although the Association of American Feed Control Officials (AAFCO) does not yet have a formal definition for this phrase, they have accepted its use on pet food labels provided the following standard is met:

"...the term "human grade" represents the product to be human edible. For a product to be human edible, all ingredients in the product must be human edible and the product must be manufactured, packed and held in accordance with federal regulations in 21 CFR 110, Current Good Manufacturing Practice in Manufacturing, Packing, or Holding Human Food."

The AAFCO Official Publication (2020)

Human-Grade Claims: The AAFCO requirement sets the bar very high for including the term human grade on a pet food label. Still, a number of companies *are* meeting this standard and are producing human-grade dog foods of a variety of types, including dehydrated, cold-pressed kibble, and fresh cooked/frozen. The underlying assumption with all foods that carry a human-grade claim is that because of the types of ingredients, regulatory oversight, sanitation methods, and processing that are used, the end product will be safer and of greater nutritional quality than other foods that do not carry a human-grade claim.

What Do We Know? However, do we know this to be true? Well, there are some published data showing that human-grade chicken ingredients are of higher quality compared with the rendered chicken meals that are typically used in extruded dog foods. In addition, we also have three studies that compared the nutritional value of commercial, human-grade, dog foods to that of traditional foods produced with pet-grade ingredients. Let's look at what they have found:

181

Study 1: The nutrient digestibility and energy content of a set of six commercially produced, human-grade, fresh-cooked dog foods were tested using a validated feeding assay (1). Each food included a different primary protein source (beef, chicken, fish, lamb, turkey, or venison) plus a digestible starch source (potato, rice, squash, or macaroni).

Results: Although the foods were produced by the same company, there were several significant differences among the six products:

🐾 *Total (dry matter) digestibility:* The overall digestibility values were moderate for three of the six foods – those containing chicken, turkey, or lamb, with values between 78 and 82 percent. However, the digestibility values for the fish and venison diets were quite low – around 67 percent. In the dog food world, digestibility values less than 70 percent are considered to be quite low (and not a good thing). For example, dry matter digestibility values that have been reported for extruded dry foods (*not* made with human-grade ingredients) typically range between 64 percent (low) to 85 percent of greater (high). Therefore, while the human-grade chicken, turkey and lamb foods in this study are considered to be moderately high in digestibility, the venison and fish foods had very low values – and certainly did not fare better than typical extruded foods made with pet-grade ingredients.

🐾 *Indispensable (essential) amino acid digestibility:* Taken together, the digestibility values for all of the essential amino acids provides a measure of a food's protein quality. Interestingly, the amino acid digestibility values of these foods were all quite high, ranging between 79 and 93 percent. These values, on average, are higher than those typically reported for commercial dry dog foods made with pet-grade ingredients. What this means, practically speaking, is that while the foods were only moderately digestible overall, their protein sources and amino acid profiles reflect high quality protein sources and indispensable amino acid availability. *So, what gives?*

🐾 ***Dietary fiber:*** One explanation may have to do with the dietary fiber content of the products. There were wide differences in total dietary fiber content among the six foods (between 4 and 14 percent). These differences were caused by the different carbohydrate sources used and may have accounted, at least in part, for the lower dry matter digestibilities (without a loss of protein digestibility) in the fish and venison foods. This effect was not considered to be detrimental by the researchers, since dietary fiber provides several gastrointestinal benefits to dogs.

Conclusions: The researchers reported amino acid availability values that were very high, indicating that the human-grade products included high quality protein sources. However, while this study provided valuable information, it was not a feeding study with dogs. Rather, it used an assay that is correlated with dog data. In addition, the study did not directly compare the human-grade products with commercial foods made with pet-grade ingredients.

Study 2: A subsequent study by the same group of researchers compared two fresh-cooked human-grade foods to a pet-grade extruded food and a pet-grade fresh-cooked food in a 28-day feeding study with dogs (2). They measured fecal characteristics, nutrient digestibilities, gut microbiota/metabolites, and standard blood serum health measurements.

Results: Several significant findings were found when the four foods were compared:

🐾 *Acceptance:* The dogs readily consumed all four of the foods and remained healthy throughout the study period. However, dogs needed to eat significantly more of the extruded dry dog food to maintain optimal body weight and condition compared to the other three foods.

🐾 *Digestibility differences*: The digestibility values (dry matter, organic matter, and fat) of the two human-grade foods were significantly greater than the digestibility values of both types of pet-grade products. For example, dry matter digestibility was 91 percent for both of the human-grade foods compared to a value of 81.5 percent for the extruded dry dog food. Similar differences were found among protein digestibility values.

🐾 *The Scoop on poop*: All four of the products resulted in optimal stool quality scores. However, feeding the human-grade products resulted in lower total fecal output when compared with feeding the extruded or fresh-cooked pet-grade foods.

Study 3: The third study compared the performance of four varieties of human-grade dog foods produced by a single company to a chicken-based extruded dry dog food (3). Dogs were fed each food for a period of 10 days. Collected data included measures of digestibility, energy, and fecal quality.

Results: Science loves replication and the results of this study were similar to earlier work:

🐾 *Digestibility values:* When fed to dogs, the extruded kibble had significantly lower dry matter, protein, fat and NFE (an estimate of carbohydrates) digestibility values compared with all four of the fresh-cooked human-grade products. The differences were dramatic. For example, dry matter digestibility of the kibble was ~ 82 percent, while the digestibility values of all four fresh-cooked foods were 90 percent or higher.

🐾 *Protein:* Similarly, the protein digestibility of the kibble was about 85 percent. Protein digestibility values for the four

184

fresh foods were between **92 and 94 percent** (rock star values, once again).

🐾 *Feces*: Dogs fed the human-grade, fresh-cooked foods had significantly lower defecation frequencies (numbers of poops per day) and lower fecal volumes than when they were fed the dry kibble.

Take Away for Dog Folks: Collectively, the results of these three research studies tell us that the protein quality of the human-grade foods was superior to values that we typically see in extruded, dry dog foods. Two of the three studies also found superior dry matter (total) digestibility values for the human-grade foods as well.

The high values for the human-grade foods are likely a result of both ingredient quality (human-grade vs. pet-grade) and processing method (gentle cooking vs. extrusion). These two factors are difficult to separate because most of the human-grade foods that are commercially produced are also less highly processed than traditional pet foods. Study 2 gives us a bit of insight into these different influences. The fresh-cooked product was produced using less heat/mechanical processing when compared with the extruded food, and both products used pet-grade ingredients. The results showed that the pet-grade fresh-cooked food had intermediate digestibility values, between the human-grade foods and the extruded food, suggesting a significant effect of processing. (We explore the effects of food processing on the nutrient value in dog foods in more detail in the following chapter).

Of course, there are reasons other than and in addition to nutrient digestibility and protein quality that dog owners may choose a human-grade dog food. These include ingredient sourcing and handling, quality control, regulatory oversight, the use of Good Manufacturing Practices, and product safety – all of which can be important factors when selecting a dog food. For now, we have at least some evidence suggesting that foods made with human-grade ingredients that are produced with minimal processing perform very well when fed to dogs. This is information that dog owners can use when evaluating and selecting healthful foods for their dogs.

Cited Studies:

1. Oba PM, Utterback PL, Parsons CM, Swanson KS: True nutrient and amino acid digestibility of dog foods made with human-grade ingredients using the precision-fed cecectomized rooster assay. *Journal of Animal Science* 2020; 4:442-451.

2. Do S, Phungviwatniku T, de Godoy MRC, Swanson KS. Nutrient digestibility and fecal characteristics, microbiota, and metabolites in dogs fed human-grade foods. *Journal of Animal Sciences* 2021; 99 (2); skab028, https://doi.org/10.1093/jas/skab028.

3. Tanprasertsuk J, Perry LM, Tate DE, Honaker RW, Shmalberg J. Apparent total tract nutrient digestibility and metabolizable energy estimation in commercial fresh and extruded dry kibble dog foods. 2021; *Translational Animal Science*, Volume 5, txab071, https://doi.org/10.1093/tas/txab071.

31. Does processing affect the protein quality of dog foods?

The heat treatment that is used to produce many commercial dog foods has well-established benefits. Cooking functions to improve a food's overall digestibility, enhances a product's shelf life, and when it leads to product sterilization, assures food safety. These benefits are exactly the same that we enjoy with highly processed human foods such as canned goods, processed lunch meats and extruded cereals. However, just as with human foods, the heat and mechanical processing that is used with pet foods can lead to a loss of nutrients and can damage the food's protein. How does this occur, and should we be concerned about it?

Maillard Reaction: One of the most extensively studied processing impacts on food protein is called the Maillard reaction. This thermal process is named for the French scientist Louis Camille Maillard. In the early 1900's, the ever-enterprising Louie was attempting to produce synthetic meat protein in his laboratory. The glop that he ended up creating looked nothing at all like meat, but it did have a very distinctive meaty aroma and flavor – that of charred meat or burnt toast.

The compounds that produce these smells and flavors were eventually referred to as Maillard end products. They comprise a diverse group of cross-linked molecules formed by the binding of simple sugars (glucose, fructose, galactose) with the amino group of certain amino acids in proteins, in particular, the essential amino acid, lysine.

Charred Meat = Maillard Reaction End Products

Importance of Lysine: Lysine is one of the 10 essential amino acids (the building blocks of proteins) that must be provided in a dog's diet. The term *essential* means that dogs cannot produce these amino acids endogenously (in the body) and so they must be supplied by the protein in the food. Of the essential amino acids, lysine is rather unique in that it has a reactive amino group (the H2N and floating H in the graphic below). This group, in particular the H+ is reactive, meaning that it readily links with other molecules.

$$\text{H}_2\text{N} \quad \overset{\text{H}}{\underset{\text{O}}{\bigg|}} \quad \overset{\text{NH}_2}{\text{OH}}$$

Molecular Structure of Lysine

Heat treatment of food proteins greatly enhances the likelihood that a protein's lysine will bind with sugars and other amino acids, resulting in the production of Maillard end products. When this occurs, the altered form of lysine is not available for use by the body, even after it has been digested and absorbed into the

188

body. Maillard end products and the altered lysine they contain may be modified further to produce compounds called Advanced Glycation End products or AGEs, which have some unique properties as well (more about these below).

Because lysine is an essential amino acid, the loss of available lysine in a pet food due to the Maillard reaction is significant because it can result in lysine deficiency in foods that are formulated and promoted as providing complete and balanced nutrition. Nutritionally, this has the potential to be a serious problem.

Reactive Lysine in Dog Food: Determining the amount of reactive (available) lysine and Maillard end products in a pet food provides a useful measure of a food's protein quality. This goes above and beyond digestibility because the amount of reactive lysine reflects the actual nutritive value of the protein once it has been digested and absorbed into the body. The degree of Maillard damage can be accurately measured using a laboratory procedure that analyzes both reactive (available) lysine (RL) and total lysine (TL) in the food. A ratio is then calculated between these two values (RL:TL). A high ratio reflects more reactive lysine, less protein damage and higher quality protein. Conversely, a low value signifies greater loss of lysine during processing, more damage to the protein, and lower quality. Measuring this ratio in different dog foods can provide helpful information regarding the effects of thermal processing on a food's protein.

The Study: Researchers examined reactive lysine content and Maillard end products in a variety of commercial pet foods (1). They collected 67 different brands of food, formulated for different life stages. Lysine levels were measured for each, and RL:TL ratios were calculated. The researchers also compared available lysine levels in the foods to the minimum lysine requirements specified by the current *NRC Nutrient Requirements for Dog and Cats* (2).

189

Results: A wide range of RL:TL ratios was found in the products, suggesting that protein damage in commercial foods is highly variable and may be influenced by several factors:

🐾 *Processing type vs. ingredients*: Overall, as reflected by the RL:TL ratio, canned foods had less protein damage than extruded (dry) products, which had less damage than pelleted foods. However, the range of values *within* processing type was high and the values of the three categories of foods showed a lot of overlap. This suggests that source and type of ingredients may matter as much as or even more than processing.

🐾 *Ingredients:* Many of the ingredients that are used to produce pelleted and extruded foods are pre-treated with heat, drying, and grinding. For extruded foods, this refers primarily to the production of meat meals (see Chapter 13 for details). It is speculated that this processing and how well it is (or is not) controlled is an important determinant of changes in protein quality.

🐾 *Meeting lysine requirements*: Of the foods that were examined in this study, up to *23 percent* of a product's lysine was damaged and unavailable. When these losses were calculated while accounting for expected protein and lysine digestibility, some of the foods were expected to be at risk for not meeting the minimum lysine requirement of growing dogs.

Conclusions: The authors concluded: *"Ingredients and pet foods should be characterized with respect to their reactive lysine content and digestibility, to avoid limitations in the lysine supply to growing dogs"*.

Advanced Glycation End Products (AGEs): We have some evidence suggesting that the production of Maillard end products can result in the loss of available lysine, which in turn may significantly affect a food's ability to meet a dog's need for this essential amino acid. An additional health-related problem that is associated with Maillard end products is related to compounds called AGEs.

Maillard end products are not stable molecules. Once formed, they gradually rearrange into AGEs which are more chemically stable. These ultimately give rise to the melanoidins, which are the pigments that impart the brown coloring in heat-processed foods. AGEs are also formed in the body via glycation, which is the bonding of certain tissue proteins and sugars. These are called endogenous AGEs. Both dietary and endogenous AGEs contribute to the body's total AGE pool. Studies in various species, including humans, implicate that dietary AGEs in particular have a role in aging and in the development of several types of chronic inflammatory diseases (3).

Processed Foods and AGEs: Studies of human foods show that those containing the highest levels of AGEs are fried and broiled meats and fish (with fried bacon being extremely high), processed cheeses, and processed condiments such as tub margarine and mayonnaise. By comparison, foods that contain very low concentrations of AGEs are fresh fruits and vegetables. While roasting vegetables increases AGEs somewhat, concentrations in cooked vegetables are still orders of magnitude lower than those found in processed meat products. In dog foods, the process of rendering to produce animal-protein meals along with the high heat treatments that are used during extrusion and canning are associated with increased production of both Maillard end products and AGEs (4).

Although there are fewer studies of AGEs in pet foods compared with human foods, there are some published data. Starting around 2012, Charlotte van Rooijen, a researcher at Wageningen University in The Netherlands, conducted a series of studies of the Maillard reaction and AGEs in pet foods. These studies served to stimulate interest in AGEs, pet foods and health among other companion animal nutritionists and researchers (5).

The Study: Van Rooijen's work provided new insight into the levels of AGEs in commercially produced dog foods (6). Here are some of her important findings:

🐾 On average, the concentrations of AGEs in commercial pet foods are similar to concentrations found in highly processed human foods such as fast-food burgers, French fries, and margarines.

🐾 Levels in dog foods are usually higher in canned foods than in extruded foods, but there is a great deal of overlap between these food categories. Ultimately, the quality of starting ingredients plus processing temperatures and processing quality control will all influence the AGE concentrations found in a final product.

🐾 Last, and possibly most importantly, when the average intake per day of AGEs in dogs was compared with that of humans consuming a Western diet (and adjusted for differences in metabolic body weight), dogs consumed over *122 times more* of these compounds than a typical human.

Impacts on Canine Health? We know that the processing of commercial dog foods results in relatively high concentrations of Maillard end products, a loss of available lysine, and an increase AGEs in foods. The next question is to ask whether or not these compounds, when consumed at these levels, influence our dogs' long-term health. Although there is no direct evidence (yet) in dogs, high AGE consumption has been associated with an increased risk of several age-related chronic inflammatory disorders in humans. These include atherosclerosis, nephropathy (kidney disease), osteoarthritis, neurodegenerative diseases, and diabetes mellitus.

Most of these age-related diseases also occur in dogs, showing many similarities to human disease. There is also evidence that elevated levels of AGEs in tissue proteins occur in dogs diag-

192

nosed with these disorders. However, the exact causative nature, if one exists, between AGEs and these disorders in dogs has not been well studied. Regardless, collectively, the current information that we have suggests that, just as with our own diets, it is prudent to reduce our dogs' exposure to dietary AGEs by reducing or limiting the proportion of highly processed foods that we feed to them.

Cited Studies:

1. van Rooijen C, Bosch G, van der Poel AFB, Wierenga PA, Alexander L, Hendriks WH. Reactive lysine content in commercially available pet foods. *Journal of Nutritional Science* 2104; 3:e35:1-6.

2. National Research Council, National Academy of Science. *Nutrient Requirements of Dogs and Cats*, 2006 Edition, National Academies Press, Washington, DC.

3. Raditic DM. Insights into commercial pet foods. *Veterinary Clinics: Small Animal Practice* 2021; 51:551-562.

4. Gill V, Kumar V, Singh K, Kumar A, Kim J. Advanced Glycation End Products (AGEs) may be a striking link between modern diet and health (Review Paper). *Biochemicals* 2019; 9:888-904.

5. Teodorowicz M, Hendriks WH, Wichers HJ, Savelkoul HFJ. Immunomodulation by processed animal feed: The role of Maillard reaction products and Advanced Glycation End Products (AGEs). *Frontiers in Immunology* 2018; 9:2008; doi: 10:3389/fimmuno.2018.02088.

6. van Rooijen C, Bosch G, van der Poel AFB, Wierenga PA, Alexander L, Hendriks WH. The Maillard reaction and pet food processing: Effects on nutritive value and pet health. *Nutrition Research Reviews* 2013; 26:130-148.

FOODS - The Science Dog Recommends

Here are a few evidence-based tips for evaluating and selecting foods for your dog:

🐾 The term "*natural*" on a dog food package or in a brand name means only that the food does not contain artificial preservatives. Other than this, "natural" provides no information that can help owners to differentiate among foods in terms of ingredients, food quality, digestibility, manufacturing practices or food safety.

🐾 General health claims for dog foods are broadly defined, loosely regulated, and require no supporting scientific evidence. When selecting an over-the-counter food, keep your skeptic's hat firmly in place and avoid the appeal of marketing health claims.

🐾 A safe upper limit for mercury in dog foods has not been established and pet food companies are not required to test fish-containing products for this heavy metal. It is prudent to avoid feeding foods that contain fish as their primary protein source as your dog's single food source.

🐾 Most of the health-related claims that are made for feeding raw diets to dogs do not have supporting evidence. However, studies of the short-term health benefits and nutritional performance of raw foods have found that raw food performed well nutritionally and supported dog health. Regardless, evidence of *superiority* of a raw diet, especially when compared with moderately cooked foods, is lacking.

* Multiple studies report that raw, meat-based pet foods are more likely to be contaminated with bacterial pathogens than are cooked foods. Contrary to the belief that freezing raw dog food prevents microbial contamination, this assumption is not supported by research. Rather, bacteria are present at the time of thawing and will proliferate rapidly when foods are stored in the refrigerator. Owners should not rely upon freezing alone to keep a raw meat-based product free from contamination.

* In contrast to frozen raw foods, there is some evidence that the very low moisture content of freeze-dried raw dog foods significantly reduces the survival of food-borne pathogens at the point of feeding.

* High pressure processing (HPP) is an effective processing treatment used with raw pet foods that significantly reduces microbial contamination. Current evidence also shows that HPP does not diminish the nutritional value of a raw food.

* If you feed raw, consider selecting a freeze-dried product or select only frozen foods that are preserved using HPP. Select only foods that are produced by a reputable manufacturer and that have not been recalled for microbial contamination. When feeding your dog, avoid handling raw foods and always wash your hands, food preparation surfaces, and dog bowls thoroughly.

* Foods made with human-grade ingredients perform very well when fed to dogs. Tested products have had high digestibility and protein quality values, are well accepted by dogs, and result in reduced feces production. The high quality of these foods is likely to be a result of both ingredient quality (human-grade vs. pet-grade) and processing method (gentle cooking vs. extrusion).

🐾 The thermal processing that occurs during rendering to produce animal protein meals and during extrusion and canning results in a loss of available lysine, the production of Maillard end products, and increased AGEs in dog foods. Because lysine is an essential nutrient, excessive losses have the potential to lead to lysine deficiency. High AGE consumption is associated with increased risk of several forms of inflammatory disease. Just as with our own diets, it is prudent to reduce dogs' exposure to dietary AGEs by limiting the proportion of highly processed foods that they are fed.

🐾 A few general tips:

✓ Avoid feeding a single brand of food to dogs (or using a single homemade recipe) over long periods of time. Rather, select several reputable manufacturers, brands and even forms of food. Mix and rotate these foods to provide foods and ingredients from different sources and that use different formulations (recipes).

✓ Select at least some foods that are less highly processed than traditional dry (extruded) foods. If your budget allows, select one or more foods to rotate or mix that use human grade ingredients.

✓ Other factors to consider when selecting a food include ingredient source (local, domestic or out-of-country), types of quality control and food preservation measures used by the manufacturer, product safety, and the recall history of the company or brand.

✓ If using a homemade recipe, choose several (not just one) that have been balanced to meet either AAFCO nutrient profiles or NRC guidelines.

Part 5 – Feeding

32. When did we first start feeding dogs?

Traditionally, when discussing the history of dog food, we have looked back only about 160 years from present day. The story typically begins with a gentleman by the name of James Spratt (yes, that was actually his name). Around the year 1860, Spratt created a baked patty for dogs that contained a concoction of grains, beetroot, vegetables, and beef by-products. They were sold as Spratt's Dog & Puppy Cakes.

Although dogs seemed to enjoy his cakes, Spratt's marketing skills were not great and his cakes did not sell very well. Enter Carleton Ellis, an American inventor and entrepreneur who is credited with the creation of margarine, varnish, and paint remover, among other things. Ellis suggested that Spratt's cakes and other dog foods of the time should be shaped in to small, bone-shaped biscuits rather than round cakes. The biscuits were an instant hit and sales soared. The race between nutritional science and goofy marketing gimmicks in pets foods was on. To date, the marketers appear to be winning (see Chapter 21 and Chapter 22).

Knowing this history, I was surprised and intrigued to find some published research suggesting that Mr. Spratt may have been a bit late to the dog food cooking table (1). Specifically, there is evidence suggesting that humans may have started preparing and feeding foods designed for dogs much (much) earlier than the 1800s.

Early Dogs: A team of archeologists examined the remains of 27 adult dogs found in the Can Roqueta archaeological site near Barcelona, Spain. The dogs are estimated to have lived between 2500 and 3000 years ago and were buried in close proximity to human settlements. They were considered to be fully domesticated and appear to have had a variety of functions and roles in their human communities. The researchers used carbon and nitrogen stable isotope dating to study the collagen make-up of the ancient dogs' bones. Because collagen is produced in the body from dietary protein, this analysis provides several types of information regarding an individual's diet. This includes:

🐾 The animal's trophic level, meaning its place in the food chain as a primary, secondary, or tertiary consumer.

🐾 Whether the bulk of the dog's food was coming from terrestrial (land) versus marine sources, plus the proportion of animal-source protein versus plant-source protein in the diet.

🐾 The actual *types* of plants consumed based upon their patterns of photosynthetic activity, ability to fix nitrogen and classification as a domesticated cultivar versus a wild plant species.

Earlier Work: There is ample evidence that early domesticated dogs consumed diets very similar to the human populations that they lived near or with. For example, in parts of Japan and coastal areas of North America, early dogs and their humans subsisted on diets almost exclusively comprised of marine animals and plants (go omega-3 fatty acids!). Conversely, early humans and dogs living in Mesoamerica consumed diets that contained a high proportion of maize (corn), while those existing in northern hunting communities subsisted on a highly carnivorous diet. What has not been clear in many of these ancient relationships has been whether or not the humans who were cohabitating with the dogs were *intentionally* preparing food for the dogs versus the dogs' diets simply reflecting shared food scraps and scavenging behaviors. The data collected by archeologists using isotope dating provides evidence that helps to answer this question.

Results: The scientists in this study learned quite a bit about the ancient dogs and their diets:

🐾 *Evidence of breed/type differences:* Although many of the dogs were medium-sized, their morphological diversity suggested that humans were starting to select and possibly breed dogs for specific roles and functions. Within the group, there were several unusually large dogs, suggesting that some of the dogs had been developed and bred for pulling, guarding sheep and goats, or other forms of hard work.

🐾 *Varied diets:* The isotope data showed widely varied diets, with some dogs consuming a high proportion of plant-based proteins, while another subset of dogs being fed a largely carnivorous diet that was very high in meat.

🐾 *Millet vs. meat:* Further analysis classified several general groups of dogs that lined up with ethnographic information regarding the cultures and agriculture/hunting activities of their associated humans. The diversity of the dogs' diets apparently matched increasingly stratified human roles (and status) and suggested that dogs were being used (and fed) for different purposes.

🐾 *Different dogs, different foods:* The researchers suggested that the large dogs had been bred for work – herding, guarding livestock or pulling loads. This subset of dogs was fed a diet high in cultivated grains to provide a readily available and abundant source of calories. In contrast another subset of dogs (the meat eaters) may have had enjoyed a very different role in society. These dogs were thought to be associated with the higher social status of their owners (the initial traders, possibly), were associated with funeral rituals, and were buried alongside a (presumably, their) human. Rather than being fed grains, these dogs were fed a highly valued diet – one that was high in meat. Were these dogs the very first pampered pets, perhaps?

201

Conclusions: The differentiation of dogs' functions and roles during the eras studied by these researchers (late Bronze and early Iron periods) along with varied diets potentially matching these different roles, suggest that the foods fed to the dogs were intentionally prepared. The dogs' different diets may have reflected the needs of a working dog requiring high amounts of readily available calories (high grains) versus a diet fed to high-status dogs associated with similarly high-status humans. In both cases, this differentiation is suggestive of intentional preparation and feeding of a particular diet, rather than reflective of dogs simply scavenging human food scraps. In other words, the people living near Can Roqueta with their dogs, more than 2500 years ago, may have been the very first producers of dog foods.

One has to wonder if their food came in bone-shaped biscuits....

Cited Study:

1. Albizuri S, Grandal-d'Anglade A, Maroto J, Oliva M, et al. Dogs that ate plants: Changes in the canine diet during the late Bronze Age and the First Iron Age in the Northeast Iberian Peninsula. *Journal of World Prehistory* 2021; 34, 75–119.

33. Can dogs learn food preferences from their owners?

In recent years, behavior research has shown that dogs can readily learn new behaviors and even problem solve by observing the actions of another dog or human. This cognitive skill, called social learning, takes a variety of forms. Dogs can learn to follow pointing, solve food puzzles, and maneuver around barriers after simply watching a person correctly perform the task (1,2). Similarly, there is evidence that dogs who observe the training session of another dog more easily acquire some of the new behaviors demonstrated by the observed dog (3).

Social Transmission of Food Preferences: Another type of social learning involves feeding behavior and food preferences. Called *social transmission of food preferences* (STFP), this type of learning refers to the transmission of information about foods solely through olfactory cues, rather than through proximity and visual cues. In other words, Stanley may learn what is good to eat by smelling Alice's face and breath after she eats a new food rather than by actually witnessing Alice consume the food. This differs from what we know about other forms of social learning in dogs, in which *visual* observation is the primary conduit to learning the new behavior or preference.

How does STFP Work? The study of STFP has an interesting history. In the early 1980's, some innovative (or perhaps bored) researchers decided to find out if Norway rats could transmit information to one another about sources of food through scent alone. To test this, they added a novel flavor, in this case either cinnamon or cocoa, to the rat's food. One rat, who they deemed the Demonstrator (we will call him Dave), was separated from his partner rat and offered one of the foods.

After enjoying his flavored treat, Dave was reunited with his partner. The researchers labeled this rat the Observer (we shall call him Oli). Dave and Oli were allowed to have a happy reunion for 15 minutes. Oli was then removed and offered *both* foods. And guess what! Oli consistently chose the flavor of food that his pal Dave had previously enjoyed – even though this was the first time that Oli was presented with that particular flavor and even though he had not directly witnessed Dave eating the food. In repeated rounds of Dave and Oli experiments, the Oli rats consistently showed a preference for the flavor that their particular Dave had previously consumed.

Over the years, these results have been found to be robust, showing that Norway rats are quite proficient at STFP. It is speculated that this form of social learning benefits rats because it provides an effective way for individuals to learn from one another about safe vs. unsafe foods in their environment.

What about Dogs? In addition to rats, STFP has been demonstrated in mice, gerbils, rabbits, voles, and even in several primate species. However, only a couple of studies have examined the ability of dogs to learn food preferences in this way. The first, published in 2007, reported that dogs appear to be capable of learning food preferences from other dogs through scent alone and in the absence of visual cues (4). In that study, the researchers selected the novel flavors of basil and thyme, which they added to the dogs' food. Using the same protocol as the Dave and Oli experiments, they reported similar results to the rat studies.

A second, more recent study attempted to replicate the 2007 study and also asked the additional question *"Can dogs learn food preferences from their owners via STFP?"* In other words, if you come home smelling like the burger that you just enjoyed at your local pub, would your dog prefer a burger as his meal that night?

The Study: Researchers at Texas Tech University in the United States, conducted a set of three experiments (5):

🐾 *Experiment 1 – Owners and their dogs*: A group of 24 dog and owner pairs were tested. Each owner consumed a bowl of either blueberry- or strawberry-flavored oatmeal while separated from their dog. After being reunited, the dogs and owners interacted for five minutes, during which time owners encouraged their dogs to sniff their face and mouth (Note: Owners who dislike dog kisses need not apply). Following kiss-time, the dogs were allowed to smell both foods in a standard two-bowl preference test and could then consume as much of each food as they desired. *Results:* In a nutshell, unlike rats, the dogs did not care which flavor of oatmeal their owners had previously enjoyed. They consumed similar amounts of each flavor, showing no preference.

🐾 *Experiment 2 – Shelter dog pairs*: Twelve shelter dogs (6 pairs) were tested. Each pair of dogs was housed together, so they were familiar to each other. The jam flavored oatmeal test was repeated, using a dog rather than an owner as the demonstrator. Kiss-time and two-bowl preference tests were the same. *Results:* Once again, the dogs did not show a preference for the flavor that was just consumed by their dog friend. The observer dogs consumed amounts of food that were not significantly different from what they would have consumed by chance (or for my dogs, whichever oatmeal bowl happened to be closer).

🐾 *Experiment 3 – Replication of earlier study*: Given the lack of evidence for STFP provided by the first two studies, the researchers decided to carefully replicate the 2007 study that had reported food preference transmission between dogs. Instead of using fruit-flavored oatmeal, they used dog food flavored with either basil or thyme and carefully repeated the methods used in the earlier trial. *Results (Ruh roh):* The Olis in this experiment did *not* prefer the flavor of the Daves.

They basically chose in proportions that were not statistically different from chance, as in the first two experiments.

Take Away for Dog Folks: The researchers concluded that dogs do *not* appear to readily acquire a food preference (at least for strawberry versus blueberry flavored oatmeal) from either their owner or another dog. Similarly, the researchers were unable to replicate previous work that reported food preference acquisition between pairs of dogs. However, there is still a bit more to learn from this work:

🐾 *Vison vs. smell:* This set of three studies showed a lack of support for a specific type of social learning in dogs – developing a food preference based not upon *seeing* what another dog or human is eating, but rather based upon *smelling* what the dog or person had recently consumed. This is an important distinction because we have substantial evidence of social learning in dogs when they are provided with visual cues. We know that dogs are proficient at attending to and understanding cues such as body postures, emotional expressions, and eye contact. However, we also know that dogs have a highly developed and acute sense of smell and that they rely heavily upon olfaction as they go about their daily lives. For this reason, the "null" results of these studies are a bit surprising.

🐾 *Dogs vs. rats:* There are several explanations for dogs' failings at STFP in these experiments. One of the most salient is that the species in which STFP is most consistently demonstrated (mice and rats) usually live in groups, eat the same foods, and have experienced strong selective pressure for distinguishing between foods that are safe versus those that are unsafe. Perhaps this type of pressure has not existed for dogs to the same degree, or perhaps domestication-related changes have led dogs to rely more upon visual cues during observational learning.

🐾 ***Flavors tested:*** Another explanation, and one that the authors address, has to do with the attraction of the novel flavors to dogs. It is possible that the novel flavors that were used in these experiments were not yummy enough (or perhaps did not differ enough) to make an impression on the dogs. My husband and I currently live with two Goldens and a Toller. The Goldens, Cooper and Alice, like many of their clan, live by the motto *"Eat it first, hope that it stays down, adjust behavior accordingly if it does not"*. If our dogs *see* Mike or I eating they always, always, always, want a bite (actually, they want all of the food). So, perhaps a difference was not found simply because many dogs do not have very discriminating (refined?) tastes and in this way may differ from those species for whom careful food selection was evolutionarily more important for ultimate survival.

Regardless, this set of studies gets high marks for science – for reporting null results (which some researchers are loathe to do), for a well-designed and well-controlled set of experiments, and for adding to our collective knowledge regarding how dogs learn.

Cited Studies:

1. Aniello B, Alterisio A, Scandurra A, Petremolo E, Iommelli MR, Aria M. What's the point? Golden and Labrador retrievers living in kennels do not understand human pointing gestures. *Animal Cognition* 2017; May 15. doi: 10.1007/s10071-017-1098-2.

2. Kubinyi E, Pongracz P, Miklosi A. Dog as a model for studying conspecific and heterospecific social learning. *Journal of Veterinary Behavior* 2009; 4:31-41.

3. Scandurra A, Mongillo P, Marinelli L, Aria M, D'Aniello B. Conspecific observational learning by adult dogs in a training context. *Applied Animal Behaviour Science* 2016; 174:116-120.

4. Lupfer-Johnson G, Ross J. Dogs acquire food preferences from interacting with recently fed conspecifics. *Behavioural Processes* 2007; 74:104-106.

5. Mendez AD Hall NJ. Evaluating and re-evaluating intra-and inter-species social transmission of food preferences in domestic dogs. *Behavioural Processes* 2021; 191:104471.

34. Should you ask your dog which foods he most enjoys?

The taste preferences of dogs are a big deal to pet food manufacturers. After all, a food may contain quality ingredients and be highly nutritious, but it cannot benefit dogs if they refuse to eat it. Those who develop dog foods go even further than this – they test foods to ensure that not only will dogs *eat* the food, but that dogs also show that they *love* the food. So, how do pet food developers go about testing this?

Traditional Palatability Tests: All pet food companies regularly measure their product's tastiness (technically called palatability) and are especially concerned with comparing their foods to those of their competitors. Traditionally, two types of standardized tests have been used. Both of these use groups of dogs (usually kenneled dogs) and collect data for 5 or more days:

- 🐾 *Single-bowl method*: One bowl of the food that is being tested is presented to the dog and the amount of food that the dog consumes is recorded. The same food is fed for five days or longer, after which a new food may be introduced. The single-bowl test assesses overall acceptability of a product and also best mimics in-home feeding situations in which a single food is typically offered. However, a limitation is that this approach does not directly compare foods and so cannot reflect preferences or allow palatability ranking.

- 🐾 *Two-bowl method*: In this test, the dog is presented with two bowls containing different products. The speed at which the dog approaches each bowl and the quantity of food that is consumed are measured. This format, called a forced choice procedure, is presumed to measure both palatability and preference. However, a limitation is that only two products can be compared in each test.

209

The Preference Ranking Test: Although these two tests have been the pet food industry standard for many years, their limitations have led nutrition researchers to examine new approaches to measuring dogs' food preferences. One of these, called Preference Ranking takes the novel approach of using food-dispensing toys to assess multiple products or ingredients, simultaneously. Nutritionists studied this approach in a set of two different experiments (1,2).

🐾 *What is a food-dispensing toy?* Food-dispensing toys are devices designed to contain bits of food that can be manipulated and moved around by dogs to slowly release the food treats. There are a wide variety of these products available, in a range of sizes, materials, and the methods they use to deliver food. Dogs enjoy these toys not only for the tasty treats that they deliver, but also because food-dispensing toys provide environmental and mental stimulation (i.e., they are fun!).

🐾 *Teaching phase:* In the first phase, a group of 12 healthy, adult beagles were trained to anticipate different treats in a set of identical toys. The researchers used traditional Kong™ toys for their experiments. In a series of training sessions, the dogs were first allowed to sniff each toy for several seconds. The toys were then placed, in a random order, several feet away from the dog and the dog was released and allowed to play with the toys. Almost all of the dogs quickly learned that each toy contained a different type of treat and each dog developed his or her specific approach to extracting the tasty treats. (Anyone who has used food dispensing toys knows how this goes....). They used various combinations of throwing, rolling, licking, and chewing to extract the food. Personally, I bet this part of the test was a whole lot of fun for both the researchers and the dogs!

🐾 *Testing phase:* During the testing phases, the dogs were presented with toys containing baked treats comprised of either five types of fat ingredient (fish oil, butter, chicken fat, vegetable shortening, or lard); five different protein ingredients (chicken liver, fish, chicken, beef, or tofu); five starches (potato, wheat, corn, tapioca, or chickpea); or five combinations of the fat/protein/starch ingredients that were baked into a bite-sized treat. All dogs were tested on all five sets of choices. Data collected included the order of selection and the time taken to extract each type of treat from the toy.

🐾 *What did the dogs prefer?* The dogs showed some strong preferences, and these generally remained consistent over time:

✓ *Fats:* Dogs liked fish oil best and lard the least, with chicken fat landing somewhere in the center. (Who knew?)

✓ *Proteins:* Among the protein ingredients, chicken liver was a clear winner. Least liked? Tofu. (Sorry vegetarians). Chicken, again, scored right smack in the middle.

✓ *Carbs*: Taters ruled here. Potato starch was a clear winner over all of the four other choices. Least popular? Chickpeas.

✓ *Combination treats*: The treat that was composed of fish oil, liver, and potato flour was a clear winner over the other four treats. The big loser? The treat containing tofu, lard, and chickpea flour.

🐾 *Meat Protein Preferences?* The dogs were also tested using preference ranking with five types of fresh meat, cut into small cubes. The meats were beef, chicken, lamb, pork, and turkey. In addition, a panel of trained, human "sniffers" analyzed the aroma components of the five meats. Here is what the dogs (and the humans) related to the researchers:

211

- ✓ **Beef it up:** All five of the meats scored around mid-range on the 5-point scale. However, beef scored significantly better than several other meats.

- ✓ **No pork, please:** Pork was least preferred of the five meats, while turkey and lamb fell in the middle of the preference ranking.

- ✓ **Complexity rules:** Aroma analysis showed that beef had the most complex and the most intensely "meaty" aroma of the five tested meats. The dogs' preferences correlated positively with the "meaty" and "roasted" aromas reported in beef.

So Many Positives! I *love* this new preference test, for several reasons. First, from a science perspective, it changes the game plan from a forced choice test in which the dog must choose between two possibilities to a more flexible test in which, in its current iteration, the dog is given a choice of five products. The increased number of choices, plus the ability to observe and record a dog's behavior while engaging with the toys, provide for a much more nuanced type of preference testing. In addition, because small amounts of test foods are used, this test lends itself to comparing preferences of individual food ingredients, something that has rarely been studied.

Second, this test has a lot to offer in terms of animal welfare and enrichment. Most of the dogs who are enlisted for palatability tests continue to be kenneled individuals rather than dogs living in homes. Offering opportunities for training with a human handler, for the mental and physical stimulation of manipulating and playing with a food toy, and the freedom to choose and interact independently are *all* enrichment approaches that can be beneficial to the quality of life of kenneled dogs. Bravo to the creators of this test!

Last, as a trainer and nutritionist, I have frequently advocated for using in-home studies with dogs and their owners. Many canine cognition research labs have been conducting this type of research (brilliantly) for years. Nutritionists have been a bit slow getting on the bus, but there is some movement in this direction. This new preference test is a *great* fit for in-home studies. Consider that many owners, trainers, and other pet professionals regularly train their dogs to use and enjoy food-dispensing toys. Also consider that many trainers are highly interested in not only our dogs enjoyment of their food, but also in how they rank various types of treats. Offering high vs. low value treats as positive reinforcers is an approach that many of us employ regularly in our training programs. So, let's hope that one of the next studies that we see with this new preference test involves dogs living in homes with their owners, doing their own little bit for science by playing with their food toys!

Take Away for Dog Folks: So, now that you know how to do it, give the "preference ranking test" a try with your own dog! Here are the steps:

1. Select a set of identical food-dispensing toys. Start with three to 6 toys, depending upon your dog's interest and your pocketbook. These should be toys that your dog loves to engage with and that are relatively easy to extract food from.

2. Choose a set of treats or foods that you would like your dog to rank in terms of preference. Place each type in a separate toy (you can mark the toys to identify them).

3. Use a quiet area of your home or a location that you regularly use for training. Minimize distractions as much as possible. Test when you know that your dog is hungry (for Labs and Goldens, this is any time at all).

4. Ask your dog to sit. Present him with each stuffed toy, allowing him several seconds to sniff. (Once your dog understands this new game, you can skip this step). Leaving him in a sit-stay, walk ~ 8 feet away and place all of the toys in a line.

5. Release your dog and observe: (a) his level of interest in each toy; (b) the order in which he starts to extract food from the toys; (c) the time to extract food from each toy.

6. Repeat daily with the same treats, presenting them in a random order. It is important that your dog learns to expect different treats in each toy (this may take several repetitions of the test – be patient!).

7. Replications are important in science, even with an "n of 1". Over several reps, you should begin to see your dog's preferences emerge. Use this information in your training program and when using food-dispensing treats as enrichment toys with your dog. You may also be able to use this test when evaluating some of the dog foods that you wish to include in your feeding plan with your dog (see following chapter).

Cited Studies:

1. Li H, Wyant R, Aldrich G, Koppel K. Preference ranking procedure: Method validation with dogs. *Animals* 2020; 10, 710:doi:10.3390/ani100440710.

2. Tsai W, Goods E, Koppel S, Aldrich G, Koppel K. Ranking of dog preference for various cooked meats. Poster presentation; *Society of Sensory Professionals* annual meeting 2018.

35. Are food-dispensing toys a good way to feed dogs?

As we saw in the previous chapter, food-dispensing toys are popular and fun for dogs. Many trainers recommend these toys as enrichment devices, approaches to teaching dogs to accept crating and alone time, and for some dogs, as a primary feeding method. Although there is not much research regarding these toys, a group of researchers at the University of Tennessee's College of Veterinary Medicine compared the activity levels of dogs who were fed using the traditional bowl approach to dogs fed using food-dispensing toys (1).

The Study: The scientists were interested in measuring the effects of using food-dispensing toys as a primary feeding method, compared with the traditional bowl-feeding approach. They recruited a group of 26 client-owned, adult dogs, all living in homes with their owners. For periods of two weeks, the dogs were fed either from a food bowl (control) or using a popular food-dispensing toy. Because the food-dispensing toy dispensed dry kibble, only dogs that were fed dry, extruded dog foods were included in the study. Total daily activity was recorded using a validated activity monitor that was attached to the dog's collar.

Results: Twenty-four dogs successfully learned to use the food-dispensing toy and were reported by their owners to enjoy the device. When fed using the toy, the dogs increased the average amount of time that they were active per day (101.6 minutes when fed with a toy vs. 90.4 minutes when fed from a bowl), and the amount of time that they spent walking each day (94.4 minutes when fed with a toy vs. 75.1 minutes when fed with a bowl). Increasing age was associated with lower overall activity and less increase in walking minutes. Although the dogs in the study were not overweight, the authors concluded: *"Feeding toys may be helpful during weight loss programs to achieve the goal of* *increasing daily exercise duration in dogs that need to lose weight"*.

Take Away for Dog Folks: These data tell us that feeding a dog with a kibble-dispensing toy can lead to an increase in total daily activity of 10 minutes and an increase in total walking time of around 20 minutes. The authors present these numbers as percentages (12 % and 26 % respectively), which serves to enhance their perceived magnitude. However, walking around the house for an additional 20 minutes per day needs to be considered in context. These dogs were *not* out for a lovely walk in the neighborhood or playing fetch with their owner in the park during these added minutes of movement. Rather they were spending this time following a food toy around the kitchen or utility room floor. There is nothing wrong with this, of course. It is just important, in my view, to consider the entire experience of the dog, rather than simply report it as an increase in time spent being active and to then (as the researchers did) conclude that this approach is desirable for increasing activity in dogs who are overweight.

Up on My Soap Box

On the Box: I am somewhat conflicted about this study and the conclusions that the authors make. On one hand, like many trainers, I think food-dispensing toys are a handy enrichment tool. They can have great utility when used as a safety cue for home-alone training and for teaching dogs to remain on a mat or to be comfortable in a crate. For dogs who are fed dry kibble, they can also provide an enjoyable alternative to traditional

216

bowl feeding. Though not measured in this study, the mental stimulation of simply working at a toy to extract tasty treats is also considered to be a benefit by many trainers (including myself).

However, as with any training tool, even those that carry the venerated label "enrichment tool", my concern is that these devices might substitute for other forms of social interaction and exercise. According to the authors of the paper, "... *food-dispensing toys may be of specific value for increasing walking – a desirable activity in dogs undergoing treatment for obesity".* In my view, recommendations of this type could lead an owner to rationalize that their dog, via the use of a food-dispensing toy, is receiving adequate levels of exercise – even enough to help him to lose weight (!).

Subsequently, increasing dog walks or trips to the park, adding a new training activity, or playing fetch together in the yard may no longer be considered necessary. In addition to providing excellent physical exercise and mental stimulation, these activities are also highly *social* in nature. Unlike food-dispensing toys (and remember, I do like these toys....in moderation), walking, training, playing and just spending time with our dogs are all activities that we share, that increase our bond and the love that we have for our dogs, and which are mutually beneficial and enjoyable.

I have one additional point. This may seem minor, but we need to consider the many different forms of food that are fed to dogs today. I have certainly explored many of these in this book. Because most food-dispensing devices work only with dry kibble or semi-soft treats, they by design will limit the type of food that an owner can choose to feed. Today, a substantial number of owners feed no dry products at all. In these cases, the use of food-dispensing toys, except when used for training purposes, is pretty much off of the table.

Therefore, while I completely agree that these toys have use as enrichment devices and for certain training goals, and possibly as an approach to feeding (some) of a dog's meals, they should be add-ons rather than replacements for other social, and in my opinion much more valuable, interactions with our dogs.

Walking with Dogs – A Great Way to Exercise Together!

Cited Study:

1. Su Dk, Murphy M, Hand A, Zhu X, Witzel-Rollins A. Impact of feeding method on overall activity of indoor, client-owned dogs. *Journal of Small Animal Practice* 2019; Doi:10.1111/jsap.13003.

36. Are chews & foods made with gullets and necks safe?

Innovative dog chews and treats are all the rage these days. Despite the claims of their sellers, most of these products are new twists on an old theme – taking the parts of food animals that we typically discard as inedible waste and turning them into expensive and often highly sought-after dog treats. A few examples are bully sticks, pig ears, pig/cow hooves, cod skins, and the topic of this chapter, gullets (esophagus) and tracheae. In addition to coming in a dried form as a chew, the entire neck regions of beef, lamb, chicken, turkey, and other food animals are also included in some commercial and homemade raw diets.

Quick Anatomy Lesson: When a cow (or chicken or turkey) is dissected for the production of human-grade meat, the animal's trachea and esophagus are removed, become by-products, and enter the feed-grade ingredient supply stream. The thyroid gland is attached to these body parts as a small organ that wraps around the upper portion of an animal's trachea (windpipe).

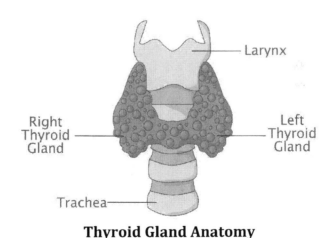

Thyroid Gland Anatomy

As feed-grade ingredients, the thyroid gland may or may not be present in tracheae by-products. Although a US law passed in 1986 prohibits the inclusion of thyroid tissue in human foods, no such law exists for by-product ingredients or pet foods. These dissected animal parts, including thyroid glands, may be included as the meat ingredient of a dog food or dried for sale as chews and treats.

Thyrotoxicosis: Including the thyroid gland in foods and chews is a health risk to dogs because thyroid tissue contains the hormone thyroxine. Neither the heat treatment of food processing or the gastric acid in a dog's stomach destroys this hormone. If included in a food or chew, thyroid hormone will be absorbed into the body and remains active. If a dog consumes enough thyroxine from the diet, an elevation in circulating thyroid hormone occurs and the dog develops thyrotoxicosis (also referred to as hyperthyroidism). Some dogs develop only elevated serum thyroxine but do not show obvious clinical signs. Others develop signs of illness that include weight loss, hyperactivity, excessive panting, and polydipsia/polyuria (increased drinking/urinating).

So, is this a common problem that owners should be concerned with? Possibly, especially if you are feeding a raw diet or if you frequently provide gullet chews to your dog.

The Evidence: The published literature includes a series of case studies of dogs affected with (and ill from) dietary thyrotoxicosis plus two pet food recalls for contamination with thyroid hormone. In both recalls, affected dogs became clinically ill and their veterinarians alerted the FDA to the problem.

🐾 *First reported cases:* Veterinarians at Justus Liebig University reported elevated plasma thyroxine levels in dogs that were being fed either a raw diet or large amounts of fresh or dried beef gullet (1). Clinical signs of hyperthyroidism were reported in half of the dogs. Following diagnosis, seven owners immediately switched to a commercial dry food and

220

stopped feeding gullet. Veterinary rechecks two weeks and again two months later revealed that plasma thyroxine concentrations had returned to normal in all dogs and clinical signs had resolved.

🐾 *Two more cases:* An 11-month-old male Rottweiler was examined for signs of weight loss, excessive panting, and increased blood thyroxine levels (2). A complete diet history revealed that the dog was being fed a commercial raw dog food. After switching the dog to another food, signs resolved, and blood thyroxine levels returned to normal. In a second case study, a two-year-old female Miniature Pinscher was examined for a failure to come into estrus (3). The dog was fed a homemade raw diet that included beef cuts from the head and neck region from a local butcher. The dog had highly elevated serum thyroxine levels. Changing the dog's diet led to normalization of serum thyroxine and normal estrus cycles.

🐾 *Chews and foods:* A study published in the Journal of the American Veterinary Medical Association reported findings of thyrotoxicosis in 14 dogs fed either a commercial raw diet or a variety of different dried chews (4). Clinical signs resolved and thyroid hormone levels were normalized within four weeks of discontinuing the suspected products. The authors were also able to obtain seven samples of the brands of food and chews. When tested, all of the products contained thyroxine. The authors state: *"The presence of high T4 [thyroxine] concentrations in a variety of pet foods or treats sold under different labels suggests that the problem of thyroid tissue contamination of such items may be widespread and not confined to only a few products or manufacturers."*

🐾 *2017 recall*: In early 2017, The FDA's Center for Veterinary Medicine (CVM) responded to veterinary reports of three dogs, living in different homes, that developed elevated serum thyroid hormone levels and clinical signs of thyrotoxicosis. The dogs were being fed one of two brands of commercial canned food. The owners were advised by their veterinarians to discontinue feeding the foods. Clinical signs disappeared and serum thyroid hormone levels returned to normal. The FDA tested the identified products, and both were found to be contaminated with thyroid hormone. The source was presumed to be beef gullets that contained thyroid gland tissue. When advised of these findings, both pet food companies initiated voluntary product recalls.

🐾 *2018 recall*: One year later, four more dogs were diagnosed with diet-induced thyrotoxicosis. The contaminated products included several varieties of one company's dried chews. Removing the treats from the dogs' diets resulted in resolution of thyrotoxicosis in all of the cases. FDA testing found the presence of thyroid hormone, presumed (again) to come from beef gullets.

🐾 *2021 paper*: A group of veterinarians and researchers examined 17 dogs that were diagnosed with thyrotoxicosis (5). They also measured thyroxine levels in the foods and chews that the dogs were fed. Both T4 (the form of thyroid hormone found circulating in blood) and T3 (the most active form of thyroid hormone) were found in the foods and treats, as well as being elevated in the serum of the dogs. Jerky treats were more likely to have elevated T4 concentrations while contaminated canned products had elevated T3. Because of T4 and T3 differences among products (and in the blood of ill dogs), the authors recommended that veterinarians who suspect diet-induced thyrotoxicosis should conduct a full thyroid test panel on patients.

Up on my Soapbox

Soapbox Time: Despite data showing that dogs are at risk of developing thyrotoxicosis if they consume foods or chews that contain thyroid hormone, despite documented cases of dietary thyrotoxicosis, and despite two commercial product recalls, there is *still* no specific regulation in the United States that prohibits the inclusion of thyroid gland tissue in pet foods or treats. *Enough is enough.* Further research is NOT needed. Rather, what we DO need is a ban on the inclusion of livestock animal thyroid glands in pet foods and treats. These are a known and demonstrated health risk to dogs.

What can an owner do? Well, first, do not feed *any* gullet chews or treats to your dog. Second, avoid feeding foods that are high in beef products as your dog's single or primary food source. If you do wish to feed beef-based foods as your dog's primary diet, your best bet is to select a product that uses only human-grade ingredients, since thyroid gland is prohibited by law from foods meant for human consumption. Last, if you are concerned, and you feed a food that you like and that your dog does well with, contact the manufacturer and ask how they ensure that their foods are not contaminated with ingredients that contain thyroid gland tissue or if they test for thyroxine in their products.

Cited Studies:

1. Kohler B, Stengel C, Neiger R. Dietary hyperthyroidism in dogs. *Journal of Small Animal Practice* 2012; 523:182-184.

2. Cornelissen S, De Roover K, Paepe D, Hesta M, Van der Meulen E, Daminet S. Dietary hyperthyroidism in a Rottweiler. *Vlaams Diergeneeskundig Tijdschrift* 2014; 83:306-311.

3. Sontas BH, Schwendenwein I, Schafer-Somi S. Primary anestrus due to dietary hyperthyroidism in a Miniature Pinscher bitch. *Canadian Veterinary Journal* 2014; 55:781-785.

4. Broome MR, Peterson ME, Kemppainen RJ, Parker VJ, Richter KP. Exogenous thyrotoxicosis in dogs attributable to consumption of all-meat commercial dog food or treats containing excessive thyroid hormone: 14 cases (2008-2013). *Journal of the American Animal Hospital Association* 2015; 246:105-111.

5. Rostein D, Jones JL, Buchweitz J, et al. Pet food-associated dietary exogenous thyrotoxicosis: Retrospective study (2016-2018) and clinical considerations. *Topics in Companion Animal Medicine* 2021; 43:1-7, dx.doi.org/ 10.1016/ j.tcam.2021. 100521.

37. Should you give rawhide chews to your dog?

A dog owner cannot walk into a pet supply store (or their own grocery store, for that matter) without noticing the explosion in the number of dog chews, dental devices and edible bones that are available for sale today. Some of these are biscuit or extruded concoctions containing a mixture of ingredients, while others originate from cow skin (rawhide chews) or are the left-over body parts of a hapless food animal, such as pig/lamb ears, pork skins, animal hooves, bully sticks, and gullets (see previous Chapter).

Even as the selection of these items has expanded, nutritional information about them is still glaringly absent. Since all of these products are intended to be chewed slowly so that pieces or the entire product will be gradually consumed by the dog, we should at least be informed as to whether these items are actually digested by dogs.

Are They Digestible? Dry matter digestibility refers to the proportion of a food that a dog's gastrointestinal tract is capable of breaking down (digesting) and absorbing into the body (see Chapter 14 for details). When we talk about the digestibility of a dog *food,* we are primarily concerned with its nutrient value and ability to nourish the dog. However, when we are considering the digestibility of rawhide treats, chews and dental products, the concerns are different but equally important. Any portion of a chew that is broken off and swallowed will travel through the length of a dog's gastrointestinal tract, just like any other food. If the dog is able to bite off large chunks or swallow an entire chew at once, that piece has the potential to cause digestive upset, impede normal gut motility, or in the worst-case scenario, cause obstruction if it is not dissolved and digested as it moves along.

Although there is limited research involving rawhide chews, a team of researchers at the University of Illinois examined the issues of digestibility by comparing several different types of dog chews, including one of the most popular forms, beef rawhide chews.

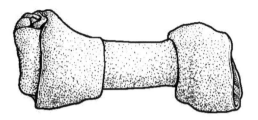

Beef Rawhide Chew

The Studies: Two experiments were conducted. The first compared the dry matter digestibilities of products from six broad categories of dog chews and treats using a laboratory method that simulates the gastric (stomach) and intestinal digestive environments of dogs (1). The second compared two types of chews, pork skin versus beef rawhides in a feeding study with healthy, adult dogs (2).

Results: Together, the two studies reported several interesting differences among the digestibility values of various types of chews:

🐾 *Pig's ears:* Chews made from pig's ears, which are composed primarily of cartilage and the protein collagen, had very low gastric (stomach) digestibilities (14%). Although the ears were almost completely digested in the intestinal environment (90%), the lack of change in the stomach means that a pig's ear treat, if swallowed whole or in a large chunk, would leave the stomach intact and enter the small intestine will little change in size or consistency.

🐾 *Beef rawhides:* Similarly, with the exception of one product, rawhide chews made from cow skin were very poorly digested in the stomach. Intestinal digestion was almost complete for one product, but all others continued to have low digestibility, even in the intestinal environment. The researchers noted that feeding rawhide chews to a dog who tends to consume large pieces might increase the dog's risk for intestinal blockage.

🐾 *Pork skin chews:* Pork skin chews were significantly more digestible than beef rawhide chews. In the stomach, the pork chew was more than 50 percent digested. In the small intestine (the major site of digestive processes), the pork skin was almost completely digested (~98%), compared with beef rawhide, which attained only 50 to 70 % digestion.

Take Away for Dog Folks: One of the most interesting results of these studies was the finding of such a large difference between the digestibility of pork skin versus beef rawhide chews. Because some dogs consume these types of chews rapidly and swallow large chunks, the fact that pork skin chews but *not* beef rawhide chews were highly degraded in the stomach and were generally well digested overall, is of significance to dog owners. These data suggest that *if* an owner is going to feed some type of rawhide chew (and mind you, I am not advocating for feeding these types of treats), but if one was choosing to do so and had a dog who might consume the treat rapidly, feeding a pork skin chew appears to be a safer bet than a beef rawhide chew.

Second, it is important to note that *all* types of rawhide-type chews are composed of collagen, a structural protein that makes up many of the connective tissues in the body. This is true for ears, pig skin, rawhide, and yes, even bully sticks. As these data show, collagen can be highly digestible (or not). The difference most likely depends on the source of the product and the type of processing that is used, both of which vary a great deal among products.

However, feeding dog a chew that is composed of collagen, even when it is highly digestible collagen, does *not* a nutritious treat make. Although collagen is an important protein in *the body, it* is not a highly nutritious *food* protein. This is because collagen is composed almost completely of non-essential amino acids and is deficient in four of the essential amino acids. What this means from a practical perspective is that even though certain types of rawhide chews are found to be highly digestible and safe (from a digestibility perspective), this does not mean that they are providing high quality nutrition to the dog. In fact, they do not.

While this research is important for pushing the peanut forward regarding the safety of these products in terms of digestibility, effects on gut motility, and risk of blockage, we still need more information (and selection) of chews for dogs that are both digestible and nutritious.

Cited Studies:

1. de Godoy MRC, Vermillion R, Bauer LL, Yamka R, Frantz N, Jia T, Fahey GC Jr, Swanson KS. *In vitro* disappearance characteristics of selected categories of commercially available dog treats. *Journal of Nutritional Science* 2014; 3:e47;1-4.

2. Hooda S, Ferreira LG, Latour MA, Bauer LL, Fahey GC Jr, Swanson KS. *In vitro* digestibility of expanded pork skin and rawhide chews, and digestion and metabolic characteristics of expanded pork skin chews in healthy adult dogs. *Journal of Animal Science* 2012; 90:4355-4361.

38. Is it more expensive to feed a homemade diet?

Homemade diets for dogs are increasingly popular. In a recent survey, 60 percent of pet owners reported that they fed their dog homemade food for at least part of their daily ration. While there are a number of arguments both for and against feeding homemade foods, a commonly held belief is that feeding homemade is significantly more costly than feeding a commercial product. Certainly, for owners of large breed dogs or in multiple pet homes, this can be a valid concern.

What Do We Know? However, do we actually know this to be true? Is feeding a commercial food always less expensive than feeding a homemade diet? There is a bit of research to help to answer this question (1).

The Study: The researchers selected two homemade dog food recipes that were formulated to provide complete and balanced nutrition for adult dogs. The recipes had been developed by canine nutritionists using a computer software program designed for balancing pet foods. For each recipe, two forms were prepared, one using chicken and one using beef as the primary protein source. The homemade foods were compared with a set of 30 brands of commercial dog food that were formulated for adult maintenance. The commercial products were divided into categories of super premium, premium and standard, based upon ingredients and cost.

The Dogs: The researchers calculated the average daily energy (kilocalorie) needs of adult dogs weighing 3, 15, 30 and 50 kilograms (6.6, 33, 66 and 110 lbs.), to represent small, medium, large and giant breed dogs. They then calculated the volume of each food needed daily to maintain a healthy body weight for dogs of these sizes. Average retail prices of the commercial foods and for ingredients of the homemade foods were used to calculate cost comparisons.

Results: The results were presented as a cost per 1000 kcal of feeding and also as cost per day for each size category of dog. The researcher note that their results were similar to those of an earlier and smaller study (2). Overall, feeding a homemade diet is expected to be slightly more expensive than feeding a commercial food, but it will not *always* be more expensive:

🐾 ***Commercial extruded dry foods are cheapest***: Overall, feeding a commercial dry (extruded) diet was less expensive than feeding a homemade food, across all three commercial food segments (super premium, premium and standard).

🐾 ***Canned foods are most expensive***: By far. When compared with commercial dry foods, on a per 1000 kcal basis, wet (canned) foods cost between 8- and 15-times more. When compared with a homemade diet, wet foods were three to four times more expensive than feeding homemade.

🐾 ***Homemade ingredients mattered***: When different primary protein sources were compared, producing a homemade food using chicken as the primary protein source was significantly less expensive than using beef.

So, What IS the Cost per Day? Here's the math:

🐾 ***The wee ones***: Naturally, feeding a tiny dog is the least expensive. Feeding a 6 lb. dog a homemade food made with chicken or beef cost between 56 and 81 cents per day, respectively. Feeding the same little fella a commercial dry food cost between (wait for it)......12 and 20 cents per day. (In other words, pretty much nuthin'). Feeding a commercial canned (wet) food, on the other hand, was the MOST expensive (surprise!) at almost two dollars per day.

- 🐾 *Mid-size eaters:* Feeding dogs who weigh between 30 and 60 lbs. is a bit more costly. If you are feeding a homemade, chicken-based food, the cost would range between approximately two and three dollars per day. Feeding a dry food? Much less expensive – about 50 cents to one dollar a day. Wet food again comes in the highest at 6 to 11 dollars per day.

- 🐾 *The big guys:* Last, feeding a homemade food to a dog who weighs 100 lbs. or more will cost between four and seven dollars a day. Commercial dry – a buck to a buck fifty and canned, up to 15 dollars per day.

Up on my Soapbox

On My Soapbox: The commercial pet food industry frequently informs pet owners that they should *not f*eed a homemade diet to their dog because (they argue) most, if not all, recipes are not well balanced and so, over time, could prove nutritionally harmful to dogs. This is simply not true.

There are multiple sources for balanced and healthy homemade foods for dogs. These include recipes that are formulated and sold by qualified pet nutritionists as well as recipes provided via pet diet software programs available for home use. Homemade diets *can* be well-formulated and healthy, provided proper care is taken in recipe selection, ingredient choice, and food preparation.

We are also told that commercial pet foods are more convenient and less expensive than feeding a homemade diet. No argument on the first point regarding convenience. However, the data in this study clearly show that:

1. Not *all* commercial products are less expensive than feeding homemade, and

2. Feeding a well-formulated, balanced homemade food to dogs is still pretty darn cheap – between 50 cents and ~ 7 bucks a day, depending on the size of the dog.

An Example: My husband and I currently share our lives with two Goldens (Ally and Cooper) and a Toller (Stanley Short Pants). Collectively, this adds up to about 145 lbs. of dog.

Cooper, Stanley, and Alice Case

Using the estimates provided by this study, we would expect to spend about 7 to 11 dollars a day (**total**) to feed all three dogs a homemade food that uses either chicken or beef as its primary

232

protein source. Conversely, if we fed the most expensive category of extruded dry food (i.e., "super-premium"), we would be spending only about two to two and a half dollars a day to feed our dogs. To put it in perspective; I can spend more than 7 bucks during a single trip to Starbucks for a coffee and a pastry. Personally, paying up to 10 dollars a day to feed my three dogs does not seem excessive to me.

Regardless, if you have hesitated to feed a homemade food to your dog because of cost, as either part or all of his daily ration, you may want to do that math for your own dog or dogs and use that information to aid in your decision.

Cited Studies:

1. Vendramini THA, Pedrinelli V, Macedo T, et al. Homemade versus extruded and wet commercial diets for dogs: Cost comparison. *PLOs ONE* 2020: 15(7) e0236672.

2. Casna BR, Shepherd ML, Delaney SJ. Cost comparison of homemade versus commercial adult maintenance canine diets. Abstract. In: *17th Annual AAVN Clinical Nutrition and Research Abstract Symposium Proceedings,* 2017.

FEEDING - The Science Dog Recommends

Here are several new facts and practical feeding tips to consider with your own dog:

🐾 It appears that we have been preparing foods for our dogs for far longer than what was previously believed. New evidence suggests that we began feeding dogs unique diets around the time that we began to actively select and breed dogs for different roles and functions.

🐾 Although dogs are known to be proficient *visual* observational learners, they do not readily form food preferences via the scent of foods that were consumed by others – either other dogs or their human companions. So, while your dog may beg mightily for that snack you are eating, chances are, he will not learn to prefer certain foods simply by smelling them on your breath!

🐾 Ask your dog which treats and foods he likes the best with a preference ranking test using food-delivery toys. You can use this test as a fun game, to rate training treats from high value to low value, and even to evaluate new foods that you are considering for your dog.

🐾 Food-dispensing toys are a handy enrichment tool that can be used for home-alone training, to teach dogs to settle on a bed or to be comfortable in a crate, and even as an approach to feeding. However, as with all enrichment devices, food-dispensing toys should be used prudently. They should not substitute for other forms of social interaction with our dogs such as dog walks and other outdoor excursions, playing together, and enjoyable training activities.

❧ There is no specific regulation in the United States that prohibits the inclusion of thyroid gland tissue in pet foods or treats. Until this changes, it is buyer beware regarding the presence of thyroid hormone in dog foods and chews that contain animal gullets and tracheae. To be safe, do not feed dried gullet chews to your dog. Avoid feeding foods that contain only beef by-products as a protein source unless you are certain that the food's ingredients do not contain thyroid gland tissue. If you are concerned or unsure, contact the food's manufacturer and ask how they ensure that their foods are not contaminated with thyroid gland tissue.

❧ If you feed rawhide chews to your dog, it is wise to select chews made from pig's skin rather than beef rawhide, especially if you have a dog who tends to break off and swallow large pieces. Remember that feeding chews that are composed of collagen are not nutritious. As a food protein, collagen is composed almost completely of non-essential amino acids and is deficient in four of the essential amino acids.

❧ If you are interested in preparing a homemade dog food as part or all of your dog's daily diet, select several balanced recipes from either a qualified pet nutritionist or by using a pet diet software program. Homemade diets can be well-formulated and healthful for dogs and are often not inordinately expensive. Proper care should always be taken in recipe selection, ingredient choice, and food preparation. As with commercial foods, rotating recipes or mixing homemade with select commercial products is also recommended.

❧ Here are a few additional feeding tips from The Science Dog:

✓ Meal-feeding premeasured amounts of food is preferred to allowing dogs to self-feed (i.e., food available at all times). Although some dogs can self-regulate intake when self-feeding is used, many will overeat and gain weight. Meal-feeding also allows careful attention

235

to a dog's daily food consumption and health. A change in your dog's interest in food or a reduction in intake will be readily noticed, which may be an indication of a medical problem.

✓ If you feed commercial dog food, choose several different brands of foods that meet your criteria for a healthful food. If your budget allows, select at least one food that is produced using human-grade ingredients and one product (or more) that is minimally processed. Mix and rotate foods over periods of days or weeks.

✓ Provide a quiet, stress-free environment to your dog during mealtime. Training dogs to eat on a feeding mat is helpful for mealtime behaviors and is especially important in multiple-dog homes. If you live with more than one dog, do not allow dogs to steal from another dog's bowl or to interfere with one another while eating.

✓ Feeding our dogs and providing them with healthful and high-quality foods is one of the many ways that we care for them and show them love. Select well and *Feed Smart* for your dog – you will both be happy for this effort! Happy feeding!

About the Author

Linda Case is a science writer, canine nutritionist, and dog trainer. She earned her B.S. in Animal Science at Cornell University and her M.S. in Canine/Feline Nutrition at the University of Illinois. Following graduate school, Linda was a lecturer in canine and feline science in the Animal Sciences Department at the University of Illinois for 15 years and then taught companion animal behavior and training at the College of Veterinary Medicine.

Linda is the author of numerous publications and eight other books, including *Dog Smart*, *Beware the Straw Man*, and *Dog Food Logic*. She owns and operates *The Science Dog Courses*, an on-line education program that provides courses and webinars to pet owners and professionals and is the author of the popular blog, *The Science Dog* (http://thesciencedog.wordpress.com; (https://courses.thesciencedog.com/)

Linda and her husband Mike currently share their lives with three amazing dogs: Cooper, Alice and Stanley, and Pete the cat. In addition to writing and teaching, Linda enjoys hiking, swimming, cycling, yoga, and gardening – all activities that she happily shares with her dogs.

Contact information:
Linda P. Case, MS
Owner, The Science Dog Courses
https://courses.thesciencedog.com/
http://thesciencedog.wordpress.com

Index

239